Business Books
- The Business That Cared About People
- 14 Minute Mentor
- TalOp Client Relationship Management
- TalOp Teams

Team Building Tools
- Team Building 20
- More Team Building 20
- Leadership 20
- Customer Experience 20
- Flash Back
- Which One and Why …
- If I Were In Charge of the World …
- Coffee Talk
- Coffee Talk 2
- BizBuzz
- TechBuzz
- EduBuzz

Team Building Facilitator Books
- TEAM Communication Activities
- TEAM Leadership Activities
- TEAM Planning Activities
- TEAM Problem Solving
- TEAM Team Building Activities
- TEAM Team Activities
- Teambuilding with Intelligence

Other Books
- Coffee Talk Special Day
- Catchin' The Carrot
- Livin' Life Large
- Father's Message in a Bottle
- Mother's Message in a Bottle
- Devon's Extraordinary Day

Copyright © Tyler Hayden, 2019

All rights reserved. The use of any part of this publication reproduced, transmitted in any form or by any means, electronic, mechanical, recorded, or otherwise, or stored in retrieval systems, without the prior written permission of the publisher is an infringement on the copyright.

Published by Tyler Hayden

PO Box 1112

Lunenburg, Nova Scotia

Canada, B0J 2C0

Cover, Illustrations and Page Design: Steven Lacey

Printed and bound in Cyberspace and USA

National Library of Canada Cataloguing in Publication

Hayden, Tyler, 1974–

The Business that Cared About People: A Leader's Guide to Team Building and Engagement Using Multiple Intelligences, by Tyler Hayden.

ISBN 978-1-897050-49-1

Management and Leadership. 2. Project Management. 3. Business. I. Title.

Join us online at **www.teambuilidngactivities.com** and find tools to help deliver great team activities and events. There is a free team building tool when you sign up for our newsletter. We would love for you to join us.

CONTENTS

Page 7 - Chapter One: Wake Up & Team Building Top 10

Meet John as he races home to his beloved grandpa. Discover the top ten things a project manager and leader needs to do to create a team.

Page 17 - Chapter Two: 2B or Not 2B and the Five Buckets

Uncover with John how choice B is the first step in becoming the steward of an amazing team. Then, explore the Five Buckets (Leadership, Innovation, Commitment, Caring, and Fun) through an art installation.

Page 27 - Chapter Three: Engage People with Their Intelligences

Explore how Multiple Intelligences have been helping to reach learners. Then, investigate with John how a simple forty-question assessment can help to uncover a gateway to engagement.

Page 35 - Chapter Four: Assess Your Team's Multiple Intelligences

Team Building is what we do with people not to people, and not engaging staff is very costly. Open the Rolodex of Team Events and explore how to use learning objectives and Multiple Intelligences to create better success in activity choice for team building and engagement.

Page 52 - Chapter Five: It's not Gambling When You Give Away Poker Chips

> Break the ice and learn ten things that lead to effective energizers for teams. Then, explore how mutual respect is the best investment to fill your employees' piggy banks with one poker chip at a time.

Page 62 - Chapter Six: Debriefing:
Finding the Value of What's Underneath

> Projects need to have a distinct beginning, middle, and end. Explore how to build engaging debriefs through Productivity Processing, experiential education, Adventure Wave, & 101 ways to improve your debrief skills.

Page 87 - Appendix A: Inside the Brain Sculpture:
Multiple Intelligences of Teams

> Explore the modalities of eight Multiple Intelligences and how to lead and manage each one as a project manager and leader in the areas of: Energizing, Communicating, Building Trust, Teaching/Coaching, and Leading/Managing. Also, discover the aptitudes and preferences of each intelligence and some tips for making it all work.

Page 127 - Appendix B: Online Tools: Multiple
Intelligences Quotient

> Apply the Multiple Intelligences Tool to discover your individual team members' MIQ fingerprint. Then, apply that fingerprint alongside the rest of the team's individual scores to discover: strengths, gaps, and opportunities for your team.

Page 133 - Appendix C: Team Building:
: Inside the Rolodex of Team Events

Invest wisely in your team-building events by applying the MIQ to your selection of team events. Use this tagged tool to find your team's best fit team-building events and activities. Couple that with categorized learning objectives and improved application of team building to your project team.

Page 215 - Appendix D: Icebreakers:
: Breaking the Ice and Energizing Your Team

Further your application of MIQ in choosing energizing icebreakers. Find a link to tools online that you can download to make the professional application that much easier and more effective at www.teambuildingactivities.com/MIQtool.

Page 243 - Appendix E: The Piggy Bank: Rewarding,
: Recognizing, and Appreciating with Intelligence

Explore this toolkit filled with ideas for applying rewards, recognition, and appreciation techniques that align with MIQ.

Page 263 - Appendix F: Debriefing: Learning with Intelligence

Uncover a toolkit jam-packed with innovative debriefing tools that have been connected to MIQ so that you improve your ability to reach learners effectively and efficiently.

"Wake Up" and Team Building Top 10

"Excuse me, sir. You'll need to bring your seat back up. We're preparing to land," a soft voice whispered in my ear.

There is only one thing more uncomfortable than a red-eye flight: a transcontinental red-eye flight. Forcing my eyes open, I worked up the best smile I could manage and said, "Of course, thank you…" I strained to read her name tag, "Sandy." My grandpa always says it's important to use people's first names when you can—and my grandpa knows so much about building great engagement with people. It is the cornerstone of our family business.

Pulling myself together, I slowly lifted the in-flight magazine from my chest. I had fallen asleep reading the top 10 list they had published about our family business. It was Grandpa's Top Ten Things Managers Can Do to Build a Team. These were the guiding principles we used because, as Granddad says, "It doesn't matter what business you are in, you're a success if you have the right people doing the right things."

I glanced over the list again, always good to have a refresher on something this important to the company, and probably a stroke of luck that it was published here given why I'm rushing home.

1. Take time early on to welcome your team on-board.

Understand that every time a new person joins the team, the team dynamics will change. Take a few moments to welcome and introduce everyone (whether it's your first time together or just one person is joining for the first time). Create a clear start or launch; team relationships are key to sustainable team building.

2. Establish a clear purpose.

A team needs to have a clear and undeniable purpose. That purpose is like an umbrella under which all activity happens. As the leader, you need to protect the team from "other things" that will attempt to find space under your umbrella. A team with a clear purpose will be more efficient and effective in realizing results.

3. Develop trust and cooperation among your team members.

Trust is the cornerstone to an effective team. Trust is built progressively, so build in opportunities early on for team members to achieve outcomes. Achieving these quick goals will demonstrate individuals' strengths through contribution and create trust through productive, progressive successes (as well as identify gaps). These small achievements will also initiate momentum and energy within the team toward its purpose.

4. Develop interpersonal relationship understanding.

Team building is often achieved through "stickiness" of people. This adhesion to one another comes in lots of ways. One is adversity (gulp, we don't want that) and another is through the strategic development of interpersonal relationships. This can be accomplished by engaging in team-building activities for fun, structured learning, and even through project-based work. Check out our store for some great team-building activities that can help you achieve this outcome.

5. Establish group norms and expectations early on.

Always take time early on in the formation of your team to spend some time agreeing to ways in which the team will function. Essentially you are building a team service-level agreement around things like: how we communicate, time frames, how consensus is built, and what are the "ground rules" of being on this team. In addition, team designers can spend time investigating and agreeing to behavioural expectations like: trust, listening, safety, etc. A great tool for that is the Full Value Contract (a tool that helps build your Project Charter).

6. Develop a safe place to share ideas and information.

Communication is the lifeblood to your team. The desire to share ideas, knowledge, experience, etc., is often the tipping point between a successful team/project and a flop. As the manager or team designer it is your job to ensure that everyone feels comfortable with sharing and that the other team members respond appropriately.

7. Authentic engagement starts with you.

It seems that humanity will always rise to the lowest common denominator. When building a team, you need to set the stage and pace for acceptable outcomes within your team. Setting that bar in a challenging but achievable spot in the beginning is vital. Then, as you progress and gain momentum, challenge your team to inch the bar higher and higher. Engagement is not a destination but rather a collective investment of pushing/pulling for more.

8. Get out of the way (after a bit).

Team building happens not exclusively by implementing great activities together. It happens organically when you frame opportunities for the team to realize results, sometimes through stress and adversity. One of the ways that you can help to facilitate this is to lead as more of a consultant while your team is "problem-solving." If the team always has you resolving the issues, they will not develop "stickiness" or grow transferrable skills for future issues.

9. Keep track of the undercurrent that can rip you into very deep water.

Your team members are people. People have feelings. Not everyone is great at sharing their feelings. Some people's feelings will get the better of them and begin to cause issues for you if they get upset. Keep track of how people are feeling; get to know your team and their individual feelings. Being proactive in managing these feelings will pay long-term dividends.

10. Time is a key measure for teams.

There are lots of great measures to gauge if your team is successful (i.e., dollars sold, memberships achieved, etc.). But as a team designer time is your biggest consideration for team building. Understand when it is time to inspire your team, time to reign in your team, time to adjourn the team, etc. Ineffective teams have had their time disrespected at some point within their development—right timing what you do as a leader will be the single biggest influence in your team-building success.

I gathered my backpack, slipped my shabby iPod back into my pocket, and slid on my fleece jacket. This has been a common ritual for me over the past few months as I have been backpacking through some of the most beautiful places in Europe, Africa, and the Middle East. From having a relaxing Turkish bath in Turkey to canyoning in the Swiss Alps, it has been the adventure of a lifetime. It was part of the plan before I transitioned into running the family business.

They say timing is everything. I knew I'd have to come home. But I didn't think it would be under these circumstances.

"Thank you for flying with us," Sandy said as I shuffled my way off the plane with the other weary travellers. I'm sure the deplaning that day looked like a scene from the *Night of the Living Dead*.

"Thank you, Sandy," I said, contorting my face muscles into a smile.

As I headed down the escalator I saw a man holding a sign that read, *Mr. John Gaynor*. That's me.

"Hey man, I'm John," I said in a groggy voice. The man greeted me with a rather odd look. A super critical eye, like I was disappointing him. I guessed not shaving, showering, and wearing the same clothes for the last week might have something to do with it. You see, I got the news when I was half way through a camel expedition into the Sahara Desert. I travelled two days straight to the closest airport and bought the first ticket home. So, I guess I must have been a bit stinky and dishevelled—I guess I would've been disappointed in me, too, if I hadn't been so friggin' tired.

We hopped into the man's limo, leaving the airport and all its weary travellers trying to sort themselves out.

As we crested the hill toward town, the sun was rising beautifully over the Atlantic Ocean. You could see the small fishing boats floating on the glassy water. Heading down Main Street, the shops were still closed, well, all except Tim Hortons coffee shop, but I don't think it ever closes. We passed a few familiar faces, people out for their early morning walk with their dogs. Nice to be home.

As we pulled into the hospital parking lot, my stomach began to turn over.

I grabbed my backpack, iPod still in my pocket and fleece still on, I opened the car door at the main entrance. I moved quickly up the ramp and through the doors. Straight to the elevator and up it went.

I don't feel quite ready, I thought to myself. How do I stop this thing? I recalled the last moment I saw Grandpa. He dropped me off at the airport for my overseas adventure. He gave me the biggest, warmest hug—hugs were his signature. The doors opened.

"Is that you Indiana Jones?" I heard a familiar voice come from a chair on my left. It was my brother, well not really my brother but a friend I would consider as close as family; you know what I'm saying.

"Todd!" I said.

"Well, I heard your footsteps and knew right away it was you." Todd is legally blind, and he is the best lawyer around. That's not just my opinion. He's been headhunted by the biggest firms in the city, but he is so loyal to Grandpa that he refuses to go.

"How is Grandpa?" I asked, knowing that Todd would be the only one who wouldn't sugar-coat things for me.

"It's not good; last night was the worst yet. I think he was trying to wait till you got home. But about an hour ago…he passed."

I walked into Grandpa's room. It was surreal. The nurse pulled the sheet back that was pulled over his head. The most powerful and dynamic person I'd ever known lay lifeless and grey. I wasn't sure what kept him alive in those final hours. Was it the myriad high-tech machinery surrounding his bed or the strength of character that lived in his every cell?

Otherwise, the room was empty.

"Everyone has gone back to the house," Todd said. "Grandpa asked me to stay here and wait for you. His final words were, 'Tell John I love him, and give him this.'" Todd passed me Grandpa's iPhone. "He said to remind you that it's your turn, and that you have a busy day of meetings at the shop so don't hang around here feeling sorry for a 'dead old man.' Then he laughed and coughed."

Grandpa always liked to joke around, even while he was dying, it seems. What a great man. I sat there beside him for some time, unsure what to do next.

I took the phone Todd had given to me and headed to the chapel in the hospital. I needed a few moments to myself to cry, if I hadn't already done enough in his room.

As I gazed up at the stained-glass window that was so beautifully backlit. I recognized it as the one that Grandpa had donated to the hospital after the tragedy that took my father's life. There was a little plaque that read, For *God loved the world so much that he gave his only Son. John 3:16.*

The iPhone began to vibrate. The screen illuminated and I clicked a link to a video that immediately began to play. It was Grandpa in his hospital room.

"Well John I guess you're here and I'm not," Grandpa said, laughing.

"I'm sorry for getting in the way of your travels, I know you only had a couple of weeks left till you had to come home to execute the knowledge management plan and transfer control of the family business to you.

You know how important our company is to not only our family but also the hundreds of families in our community that work to support our efforts. I had to have Todd call you back because there are too many people's livelihoods at risk with my passing.

Our company, as you know, is in major evolution into an online powerhouse. Now is the time for strong leadership. And I guess a force greater than you or I has decided that I need to be removed from the president's chair to make way for you. I guess it's the higher force's way of making sure that I don't screw this whole 'tech' thing up," he said, laughing in between painful sounding coughs.

"So my schedule is up to date. You know me, no rest for the wicked. So dry your tears. You know I love you. You know I believe in you. You know I'll be with you forever. Now it's up to you...the business is yours."

The video stopped almost as quickly as it had started. The room was once again in total silence. Tears stained my face. I sat in total disbelief. What would I do now? Grandpa was gone.

2B or Not 2B and the Five Buckets

From behind me, I heard someone clear their throat, followed by a soft, "John?" It was the well-recognized voice of Kim, Grandpa's executive assistant. "We really need to go."

"Go?"

"Yes, Grandpa always arrived at the shop to greet the employees as they arrive at work,"

Kim said.

I looked at her, puzzled.

She said, "I miss him too. I can't believe he's gone. But you know how he is about the company. We really need to go. He would have wanted it this way."

Kim passed me one of my suits, pressed and ready to wear, and a kit of bathroom essentials. "There is a shower room at the end of this hall. You have 15 minutes. The car is waiting downstairs. I'll meet you there." Wow, I haven't worn one of these monkey suits for a long time. What am I doing? This road is going to be hard-going. There's got to be an easier way. I should just resume my travels…get away…

As I moved down the hall toward the shower, Grandpa's iPhone started to vibrate. A new screen popped up. I thought to myself, For a 78-year-old man, this guy was pretty tech savvy. The screen said, "Bear's Quote of the Day: *2B or not 2B, isn't that the eternal question? Are you going 2B or not today? Will your efforts today build a legacy never forgotten?*"

I stripped off my travel armour, and my suspicions were confirmed: I did smell pretty ripe. I quickly shaved off a few weeks' growth from my face. Jumping into the shower I felt intoxicated by the relaxing hot water caressing my back as steam billowed in the room.

*2B or not 2B…*I guess that's really what it's all about. Am I going 2B something fantastic or not? The legacies of people before me have been about who *they* are. I am who I am. The experiences and education of my life are what will shape what *I* am able to build. Am I willing to do the work required 2B the equivalent legacy of greatness not soon forgotten like that created by Grandpa, or will I decide not 2B.

If I decided to keep travelling indefinitely and not commit to the reality that is the importance of the company, I would be choosing not 2B, I thought to myself. It was time to regroup. To "get my stick on the ice" as Grandpa would say, and play this game; I knew I couldn't run away any longer. It was time to put on new armour, armour that would allow me to lead our company into a legacy "not soon forgotten," as Grandpa used to say.

I got out of the shower and etched into the steam in large writing on the mirror my commitment to myself: 2B.

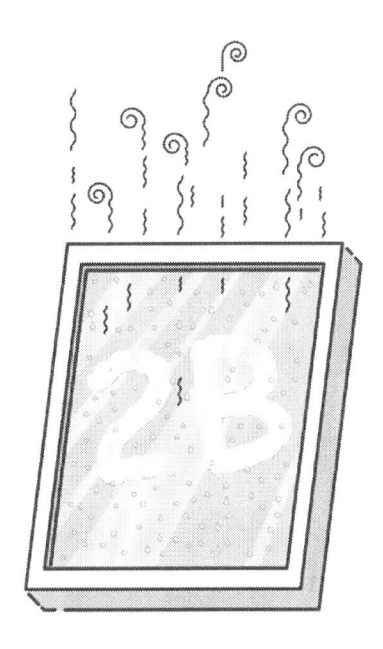

I put the travel clothes I'd been wearing for what seemed like forever into the trash can; they would be great memories, not current realities. This time I picked up a briefcase backpack that Kim had also given to me, slipped Grandpa's iPhone into my pocket and put on the suit jacket over my vest. Humph…similar routine, different adventure—same excitement. As I looked in the steamy mirror, I didn't completely recognize the blurred reflection looking back. If I'm going 2B, I've got 2B me, so I threw the jacket, pleated pants, and tie in the same trash can. I dug for a second outfit in my travel backpack, and put on my favourite jeans and kicks, and unbuttoned my vest and rolled up my shirtsleeves. That was better – I was ready 2B and 2B me.

I made my way toward the elevator, pausing briefly at Grandpa's private room door that was now closed. I touch the number on the door, 2B. "I love you Grandpa," I said and moved on toward my commitment.

Upon the high-pitched *ding* an empty elevator opened up. I headed downstairs to Kim, who was waiting for me in the car.

Kim smiled at me and said, "I'm glad you decided to come." Then, without missing a beat, she began to review the upcoming day's meetings and activities for the company. Here we go.

I watched out the car window as our driver slowly followed along the country roads I used to ride my bike on as a kid, bypassing the strawberry fields, corner store, post office, and even my bus stop. With each passing kilometre I became more nervous about what would lie behind the company doors. No doubt, everyone would be there. And be there in shock. They would be looking to me for leadership, like Grandpa said they would.

Just then, the car came to a stop. Kim stepped out first, and a moment later, stuck her head in the still open doorway to ask, "You coming?"

It took every ounce of strength I had to lift what seemed like a piano tied to my back from the back seat of the car. But somehow I lifted myself out of the car, briefcase in hand, iPhone in my pocket, and vest and jeans on—my new suit of armour. One step followed another, and still another as I confidently as possible moved toward the company entrance.

When I stopped dead, Kim spoke. "You have to open the door if you want to do this. Grandpa always opened the door."

I exhaled, grasped the handle, and opened the door. Smiling at Kim, I said, "After you."

"You're so much like Grandpa," Kim said, "chivalry first."

We walked through the main foyer, passing the security desk. "Good morning, John. I'm so sorry for your loss," said Kevin, the head of security.

"Thank you, Kevin," I replied. "And I, too, am sorry for our loss. But we'll get through this together."

Kevin smiled, but I could see the sadness behind his eyes. I knew he would miss Grandpa. Heck, Kevin was the only one who would beat Grandpa to work. He liked to have the doors unlocked as, Grandpa hated to fumble for his keys.

We walked toward the REC, otherwise known as the employees' recreation room. This was a great place where I spent a lot of time in as a child. The employees came here on their breaks, for team lunch meetings, and at the beginning of the day. Plus the room doubled as a place to inspire innovation: there was a pinball machine, jukebox, bean bags, and a fully stocked coffee bar. Grandpa loved his coffee, and teams loved to meet here.

Today's meeting, well that was a tougher one. Because of all the goings-on, I, unlike Grandpa, was late. In fact, the entire company was there before me, waiting in the REC.

The room was silent. This was ominous: 500 people sitting there, and they were all looking at me. And I didn't know what to say. I had missed welcoming everyone to work like Grandpa used to. They got here before me today; I wouldn't make that mistake tomorrow.

As I walked toward the coffee bar, Kim had the maintenance

team set up a microphone and riser for me. Man, she was good! I was so glad she was helping me out. I didn't know if I could have done this without her.

Struggling to find words, I reached into my pocket to pull out Grandpa's iPhone, thinking that by some divine intervention he would have prepared a speech for me and installed it in the memory. I fumbled a bit and hit one of the keys on the side. The camera came on and flashed a photo of the crowd in front of me. They looked at each other and began to mumble. I'm so stupid, I said to myself.

But when I looked at the photo, I noticed something. The big mural on the back wall that Grandpa had hired the local high school's art students to paint. It was a mural of an old-fashioned waterwheel with five buckets on it. Each of the five buckets was labelled with a different word: *Leadership, Innovation, Commitment, Caring,* and *Fun*.

Genius, I thought, the Five Buckets.

I began to speak from my heart. "Grandpa always told us that there are five very important things that we must do in order to ensure the sustainability of our company. Those are the Five Buckets: Leadership, Innovation, Commitment, Caring, and Fun. He told us that if we could dedicate ourselves to those Five Buckets, we could create a legacy for ourselves as well as support others in doing the same. He believed that as we filled our bucket we, too, must share the contents of our bucket for others to benefit from their power.

"The first bucket is Leadership. Leadership is a gift bestowed on a person because it is the ultimate form of trust and belief in that person and the faith of others that you will not jeopardize them. Grandpa encouraged us to utilize our leadership abilities not only inside the company but also in the community. Any opportunity to lead should be taken. 'Those leadership experiences are the marrow from which the strength of our bones comes,' he used to say.

"Innovation is the second bucket. Innovation is what keeps things fresh. We live in a world where everything is constantly changing. Yesterday, Grandpa was here in body, today in spirit. When Grandpa's grandpa opened this company, we were the premier exporter of fish products to the Commonwealth. Today, we don't fish anymore. Instead we use our business experience and global sales savvy to build an online marketing presence for countless other companies. We needed to be innovative when the fisheries began to decline. And Grandpa saw our innovative employees as the key to building a new empire. This business is now built for innovation, and you are the drivers of it.

"The bucket that defines who we are, I like to believe, is the Commitment bucket. By committing to this company and delivery of quality you are sharing the commitment that you have for your family and yourself with us. For that we are truly humbled. It is the commitment from each of you day-to-day that demonstrates we can get the job done.

"Because of how we approach Commitment we have developed a palpable culture of Caring. Caring for our internal and external customers, a sense of caring that brings people back again and again. This is our unique selling proposition—our authentic caring for the customer, each other, and our families. Grandpa used to say that here we believed in 'Santa-ology,' meaning it's up to us to share our gifts every day of the year. It is in this sharing in a humble and caring manner that we are able to move our company through any rough times, economic or tragic.

"If this were a regular morning of work, you would hear Grandpa's booming laughter echoing through the halls of this company. Grandpa was committed to making this place a Fun place to be. He recognized that you were graciously giving eight or more hours of your day to the company and its growth. He realized that this would place strains on the most important aspect of life: family. That is why Grandpa was the first to laugh, the first to take a family day, the first to do summersaults down the hallways, and even the first to wear a clown nose at a board meeting. Life should be fun. And leading a truly successful life means finding the balance between working hard and playing hard.

"I read a quote today. It said, *"2B or not 2B, isn't that the eternal question? Are you going 2B or not today. Will your efforts today build a legacy never forgotten?"* We must never forget the legacy that Grandpa has given us by remembering that today is our day 2B."

With that, there was applause. I stepped down from the riser and moved forward into the crowd that had assembled. With each worker sharing a word, a pat on my shoulder, or an acknowledging smile felt like a gentle group embrace.

I got why Grandpa loved this company: it was the people.

2BMC

Engage People with Their Intelligences

Being in the REC gave me a sense of what this was all about: I remembered why I came back, beyond Grandpa. I came back because of the people. Our company was successful as much because we worked hard at what we do – and there was not just one widget working hard, all those people in the REC work hard. I think it was Robert Griffin III who said, "Hard work beats talent any day, but if you're talented and work hard, it's hard to beat." I knew we were successful because we invested in engaging top talent so that they can achieve—win-win.

Kim and I climbed the flight of creaky stairs up to Grandpa's office. When he built the new building he carefully removed the staircase from the original building so that he could climb the stairs his father had climbed. Grandpa had said, "You need to work hard and climb every day using your talents." So, no matter how old Grandpa got, he climbed those stairs.

When I reached Grandpa's office – my office now – Kim informed me I had a 30-minute meeting with myself and softly closed the door behind her on her way out. This is probably a good thing. I've got a meeting with "my team" after that, and I've been travelling solo for so long, I'm not sure I remember how to build a team.

I finally exhaled. I looked around at the handcrafted wooden bookcases that adorned the office. Each shelf was like a unique station: particular books, treasures from travel, or photos. I remember spending time with Grandpa in his office. You see, my dad died when I was a younger man. So Grandpa made sure 2B there for me. I remember admiring the trinkets on the shelves and listening to Grandpa tell stories about how he came to find each item. He was Indiana Jones before Indiana Jones was a thing.

With that, the iPhone started to vibrate. An iCal reminder: *John, go to the shelf with the sculpture of the brain.* Grandpa surely had a plan for me.

28

> John, go to the shelf with the sculpture of the brain.

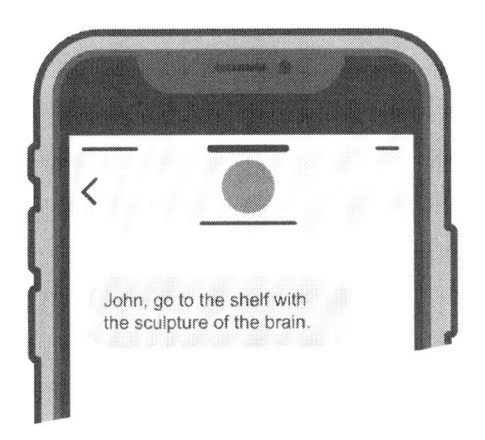

All right where's that brain? I started to scan the shelves jam-packed with Grandpa's treasures, until I landed in front of this beautiful handmade clay brain. It reminded me of the ones you'd see in a doctor's office or university lecture room. Only difference was, it wasn't that off-colour red shade that gave me the heebie-jeebies. Instead it was divided equally into eight parts and each of the parts had a different label on it.

I remembered seeing the model before but never paid it much attention. The brain sat on a pedestal that said "8 Intelligences—Howard Gardner." And under the pedestal was a stack of papers bound together with coil binding. The corners of the papers were dog-eared, and as I slid the bound stack out from under the pedestal, I could see Grandpa's handwriting all over it like graffiti on a boxcar.

When I opened the cover I found a sticky note attached to the inside with Grandpa's writing. It said, "Hey John – this is the best tool I've found for reaching our team's hearts, which was, funny enough, through their brains."

I carried the sculpture and the booklet over to Grandpa's big thinking chair. I sunk deep into its cushions, and even deeper into the words in the book.

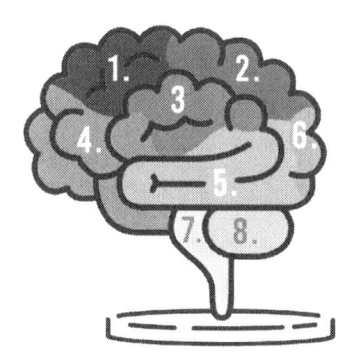

Harvard professor, Dr. Howard Gardner wrote a book called, Frames of Mind. In this book he proposes that there are major learning domains for learners in our classrooms. Quick and dirty, you tend to have "ways" that you learn best, i.e., Bodily/Kinesthetic learners learn by doing/participating/hands-on, while Mathematical Logical learners learn through numbers/strategy/logic.

About 20 years ago, I started to notice a trend in the teams I was working with and managing as a project manager under my father. Later, I continued to notice that trend when I was coaching clients on team building. I noticed that certain "occupations" liked certain events. I saw a correlation between the teams regardless of their industry, geography, maturity, etc., the connection was the "learning style." Then, as if by serendipity, my partner was doing her master's in Multiple Intelligences, and as I proofread her papers, I realized this MI could be the key to choosing team events.

I wasn't disappointed.

I looked deeper into MI and realized that those who elaborated on Gardner's work were showing "great jobs" for people who have this or that specific "learning domain strength." And guess what. When I distilled the learning outcomes and required skills of the team events I was offering, boom a stronger correlation emerged between job/team/learning styles. Design and objectives of the team-building program spoke to the learners' engagement.

In the coming pages, I'm going to share with you a more in-depth look at each learner and make suggestions for what you can do to reach and engage them. Basically, how you like to learn is the gateway to grow from; it is how people like to be managed and engaged in a team environment.

The top 8 learning styles are:

Interpersonal Learners (The "People" Learners)

Encourage discussions, presentations, mentoring. Like to work with others and can both guide and manipulate the situations to meet their needs. They love personal feedback and are very conscious of verbal and non-verbal language.

Intrapersonal Learners (The "Thinker" Learners)

Provide opportunities for self-reflection, research, and visioning. They are internally motivated and like to know how their roles connect with others. The thinkers enjoy corresponding via email. Make sure you give these people some space to work.

Bodily/Kinesthetic Learners (The "Doer" Learners)

Get ready to go! These folks like short explanations and getting involved with props and tangibles to figure out the job. They like OJT, role playing, and practising the task. They like to build models and connect their actions to everyday life.

Verbal/Linguistic Learners (The "Word" Learners)

These learners love to have things explained, both by you and by themselves for clarification. They love to present materials, put together policy handbooks, tell stories, and use humour/irony.

Visual/Spatial Learners (The "Visual" Learners)

Explore maps, charts, movies, and visioning to illustrate learning points. Encourage them to spearhead the design of displays/marketing, timelines, concept maps, documentation/handout creation.

Logical/Mathematical Learners (The "Numbers" Learners)

Logical by nature, the numbers learners like to see things in facts and figures, step-by-step, logically presented, and with short explanations. These learners will ask a lot of "why" questions and enjoy searching for the answers through experimentation.

Musical Learners (The "Music" Learners)

Probably the one you'll meet the least often in a group, they like to demonstrate things in patterns, catchy lingo, rhymes, mnemonics, and the like. They like to see the logical sequence and flow of things.

Naturalist Learners (The "Nature" Learners)

Work toward using analogies of nature to explore concepts. These folks relate to cycles, interconnectedness, patterns, cause and effect. Connect everything to real life and encourage them to classify things into their proper place.

(See Appendix A Inside the Brain Sculpture: Multiple Intelligences of Teams.)

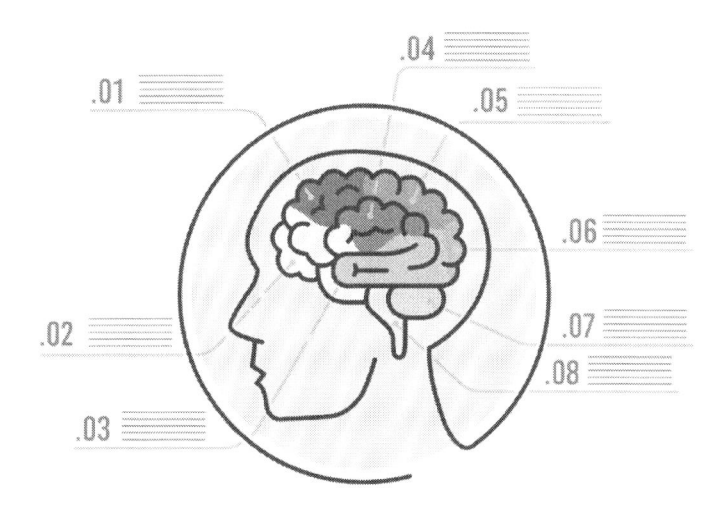

So what Grandpa is telling me is that once I have found an individual's MIQ, I can then find projects, functions, and jobs within the business or team venture that matters most to them. When work matters to people, they are more likely to engage in that work. Also, through a better understanding of our people's MIQ and how those overlap, I can know how to best reach our teams in terms of team-building events, who should be on ad hoc committees, how to reward and recognize people, and so much more.

And with that, the office door opened. Kim said, "Sir, are you ready for your meeting?"

I returned the sculpture of the brain to its shelf. "That's the key to it all, your Grandpa said," Kim remarked, looking at the model. "People like to do things the way people like to do things. If you can reach, connect, and engage with them where they comfortably do well, you are charting a course for success."

"He did like sailing analogies…the salt was in his blood," I said. "OK, let's do that meeting."

Assess Your Team's Multiple Intelligences

I walked in to the boardroom. What a fantastic view it had of our beautiful little town of Lunenburg. I'm not sure how someone could focus in this room with those vistas of the historic town, tall ships in full sail in season, and then of course the golf course. I decided to sit with my back to the window; I was still kinda in travel mode—don't want to get distracted.

"Hey John, sorry about your grandpa," said Tait after I had taken my seat

"Yeah, he was a great man," echoed Breton.

"Thank you," I said, "we are all going to miss him very much.

I understand, Tait and Breton, you've been working on a very special project. My grandpa spoke highly of the work you are doing. He trusted you both. It seemed every time I spoke with him while I was away, he was letting me know how excited he was about the new online tool you were developing for www.teambuildingactivities.com."

"Thank you. It was his pet project, for sure," said Breton.

"Yes, an online store where he could share some of the amazing tools we've been using for years here with our teams," said Tait.

"And most importantly the simple assessment tool we use to help our leaders figure out the Multiple Intelligences of their teams," Breton said. "We called it MIQ, Multiple Intelligence Quotient. It's like finding out your IQ, except for whole teams."

I said, "All right, let's do it. Bring me up to speed on this MIQ."

"The MIQ is a simple and informative tool that any manager can use. It simply takes their team through a series of forty questions. Like any self-assessment tool, it has its limitations and of course is by no means an exact science. But, as each team member weighs their answers to the questions based on their level of preference, it is possible to establish the individual's relative strengths in each of the top eight Multiple Intelligences," Breton said.

"That's right," said Tait. "And by using the information garnered over years of research and the works of Howard Gardner, the tool uses known preferences to question team members and establish their anticipated level of strength in a particular intelligence. For example, on a scale of 1 (*I'm never like that*) to 5 (*I'm always like that*) rate the following statement: 'I make friends easily.' The team member's response to this question is added to four other preference questions for that same intelligence. Simply put, the higher the score on those five questions, the higher the self-assessed acuity within that intelligence."

Tait continued, "We then plot all eight of the intelligences on what we call an MIQ fingerprint. Basically, we export the results as a spider chart to express that individual's fingerprint, and their three top intelligences. These top three enable our leaders and project managers to choose how best to approach that team member.

"It gets better. From there, we can aggregate all the team's data and establish the top three cumulative strengths. This gives our leaders the ability to make some choices generally in how they approach the entire team."

Breton said, "But the really cool part is then they can see the gaps within the team's strengths. So depending on the task, new members can be brought in, pieces outsourced, or myriad other solutions applied. Finally, when we have exported and laid all the team members' charts on top of one another, we can make educated choices based on declared intelligences of our teams, which allows us to see these things."

I looked up at the big projection screen they had turned on as they spoke, and saw a list as long as my arm that included:

√ Choose team events.

√ Choose our team based on how we complement each other's strengths.

√ Choose approaches to reduce stress.

√ Choose rewards, recognitions, and appreciations.

√ Choose ad hoc or project teams.

√ Choose meeting debriefs and icebreakers.

√ Choose training events.

√ Choose approach to negotiate change.

√ Choose new supervisors.

√ Choose message delivery.

√ Choose communication plans.

√ Choose discipline strategies.

√ Choose how to facilitate, direct, or delegate work.

"The tool of Multiple Intelligences has been used for years in schools to help teachers find the best ways of engaging individual children in the ways that classroom learning is presented," Tait said. "John, your Grandpa simply saw the correlation between how we learn and how we perform and become engaged at work."

"That's right," Breton continued. "This technique reaches into and inspires our workforce to lead from within and helps our leaders to connect with and engage their work teams in ways that draw them closer to the company and the its projects through solid 'team centric' leadership."

"Team centric," I said, "I like the sound of that. Putting the team and its collective bench strength at the centre of the action. This will help to make sure that, like Jim Collins says, 'you have the right people on the bus, sitting in the right seats.' I love what you guys did! So what's next?"

Breton piped up, "Well, head over to the site at www.teambuildingactivities.com/MIQtool and give it a try for yourself. You can self-assess your MIQ, download the tool, and apply it to teams you work with. And with that information you can start to choose team building, debriefs, reward strategies, communication styles, and so much more."

"I'll do that!" I said. "Can I look at it now?"

"We thought you'd want to," Tait said, smiling, "so we printed a copy for you."

I thanked this amazing duo for all their hard work. And with that I couldn't help myself, I was like a kid in a candy store, and I began devouring the MIQ self-test material.

———————————

Team Building with Intelligence: MIQ Self-Test

Rate the following statements according to the scale below

(5 = I'm always like that, to 1 = I'm never like that) in the blank column. The higher the numbers on your score card below the greater the intelligence in that area.

5 = I'm always like that.

4 = I'm often like that.

3 = I'm sometimes like that.

2 = I'm rarely like that.

1 = I'm never like that.

1		I love to move around while I work.
2		I get easily distracted by external noise.
3		I easily see things from other people's perspectives.
4		I am keenly aware of my personal strengths and weaknesses.
5		I love to write with a computer or by hand, on paper.
6		I like to do logic puzzles and brainteasers.
7		I am keenly interested in caring for the planet and actively recycle, compost, etc.

8	I like to explain and learn things using diagrams, maps, or illustrations.
9	I like to make my decisions based on numbers.
10	I like to daydream.
11	I like to decorate and design rooms.
12	I can easily find the irony or humour in situations.
13	I like to categorize and discriminate between things based on their characteristics.
14	I learn the tasks of the job best by doing them.
15	I can make music by playing instruments like piano, guitar, etc.
16	I love being a mentor, and being mentored.
17	I love telling jokes and stories.
18	I love a catchy rhyme or jingle to help remember things.
19	I love to play sports and be physically active.
20	I love to problem-solve and troubleshoot.
21	I easily understand the cause and effect of things.
22	I often think in terms of movies and pictures.
23	I like to make sure that everyone is heard in a group discussion.
24	I enjoy the visioning part of business/tasks.

25	I like spending time in nature, i.e., gardening, camping, birdwatching.
26	I like to draw and doodle.
27	I love to make a playlist of music that expresses how I'm feeling.
28	I love to spend time reading books and magazines.
29	I enjoy analyzing and measuring things.
30	I love planning group activities.
31	I get fidgety if I sit for too long.
32	I like to research the best ways to do things before taking action.
33	I enjoy making things, i.e., construction, models, cooking.
34	I make new friends easily.
35	I like to write down instructions, and I'm really good at it.
36	I like a strategy toward accomplishing things.
37	I like spending time by myself.
38	I can "hear" what people are saying by the tone of their voice.
39	I love to build processes to get things done.
40	I can see how to pack equipment or a car so everything fits perfectly.

MIQ – Score Card

Add up the value you gave for all the questions. Place your total score in the third column, below. Then plot your answers on the MIQ Fingerprint graphic.

Bodily Kinesthetic	1, 14, 19, 31, 33	
Musical	2, 15, 18, 27, 38	
Interpersonal	3, 16, 23, 30, 34	
Intrapersonal	4, 10, 24, 32, 37	
Logical/Mathematical	6, 9, 20, 29, 36	
Naturalistic	7, 13, 21, 25, 39	
Visual/Spatial	8, 11, 22, 26, 40	
Linguistic	5, 12, 17, 28, 35	

(More in Appendix B – Online Tools: Multiple Intelligences Quotient.)

As I eased back into Grandpa's big chair I could feel the effects of the red-eye starting to eat at my very last fibre of energy. It had been quite a day. I wasn't sure how I was going to get through the rest of it, and it was barely lunchtime. I closed my eyes for a second and I could see the beautiful beaches of Santorini, taste the spanakopita and the nice glass of wine to wash it down.

I began to drift away with the Mediterranean waves when the calendar on my phone rang again with a message titled, "Get up, this is important."

I swiped left, removing the annoyance so I could get a bit of rest. The phone chimed again with a new message: "I mean it."

I pushed out all the air out of my lungs, like Wim Hof preparing to take a dip in frigid waters, "Uuuff, okay, I wasn't tired anyway. What are we doing now Grandpa?" I chuckle. "You are one tenacious old man."

I click through the message on the screen this time, and there is more for me to read in the notes section.

Hey John, you have a really important meeting upcoming with the executive team. It's our annual team-building adventure. I kinda got unwell over the past few weeks and didn't have time to get it organized. So here is the MIQ fingerprint of the team, we beta tested Tait and Breton's work a few months ago. Use the data to pick from my Rolodex of Team Events from my shelf.

I headed back to the big shelf where I had found Grandpa's sculpture of the brain, what seemed like a few days ago but was only a couple of hours ago. I saw this steel-coloured Rolodex. I gently picked it up, remembering this was one of his prized possessions. I never got to play with it,… until today. I meander back to the chair that took me to dreamland to take a closer look.

It was locked. I was finally invited to explore the Rolodex of Team Events— a rite of passage in our family that usually involved a retreat getaway with the keeper of the Rolodex and the mentee. Given Grandpa's passing, that was not an option this time. I guessed he would have given me the key if we had been on retreat. I buzz Kim.

"Yes sir," I hear from the intercom—I still love this old tech.

"Ya. Hey, Kim," I said, "Grandpa left me a message to open the Rolodex of Team Events so that I could plan the executive retreat, and it's locked. I can't seem to find a," With that the door opened and in walked Kim.

"…key. You need the key for the Rolodex of Team Events," she said. With a huge smile she extended her right hand, in her tender grasp was a small key attached to a rubber chicken key chain.

"Thank you so much Kim. I don't know what I'd do without you."

"My pleasure, sir. May I ask one favour?" She grinned.

"Anything," I said.

"When you buzz the intercom, you will need to push the grey

Talk button while you speak. I couldn't hear a word you were saying," she said, smiling even more broadly now.

"Then how did you know I needed the key?" I said.

She chuckled. "You're just like your grandpa, always losing the key to the Rolodex. You have a lunch appointment at noon. If you need me, push the grey button," and she winked as she left the room.

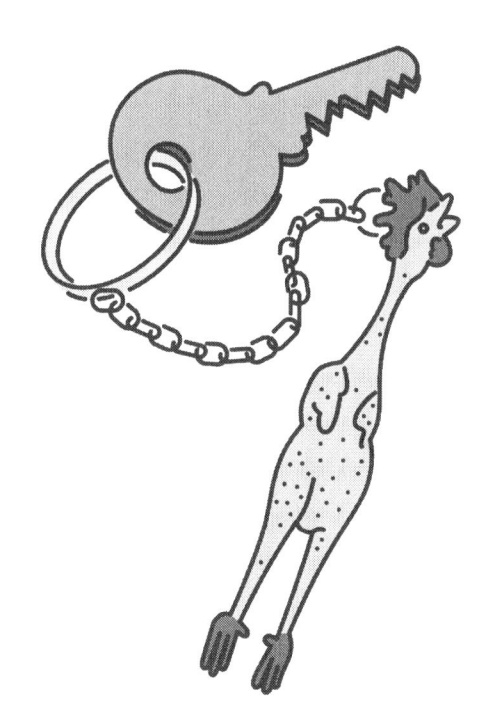

Kim is one of the great ones.

As I first rolled that steel-grey lid back, I felt like Indiana Jones discovering a precious jewel after years of searching —well, maybe it wasn't *years* of searching, thanks to Kim knowing where the key was. I really liked the rubber chicken.

Inside I saw there were several categories from "Creativity to Strategy" and "Family to Passion." Cool, so Grandpa did a lot of the work in organizing the cards into their objectives. Team building is no different than any training endeavour. You need to set out learning objectives and measures to know that you are effectively moving the needle forward; otherwise, many bean counters see team building as "fluffy." I guess they haven't read some of the statistics on employee engagement such as:

√ *Disengaged employees cost the US economy $254 to $363 billion annually. Biggest sign of disengagement is absenteeism, costing $40 billion.*

√ *Gallup polls have reported engaged workforces outperform their competition with stats like 86% higher CS ratings, 70% higher productivity, 44% greater profitability, and 78% better safety ratings.*

√ *Imagine what it would be like if you had 100 employees who gave 15% more effort on the job willingly – that's like getting fifteen free FTEs.*

√ *Motorola estimates it returns $30 for every dollar spent on professional development.*

Each section had a card dedicated to each activity. And, on each card, it told me the length of *Time* the team-building event should take, the equipment *You need* and the MIQ *Intelligences* that would resonate with the event. This is super cool! This will make choosing the team events a lot easier, just like Tait and Breton said when they showed me the MIQ tool.

I spied an envelope duct taped to the inside top of the Rolodex. I guessed there was more to it than just picking the event card and knowing the objective of the meeting and team event. I opened the envelope and began to read.

Dear John

Glad you found the key. I kept losing it, but thanks to Kim it always seemed to show up just in time, LOL. Team Building for the executive team is a labour of love for me. I love to try to pick the perfect event for our retreat. I try to match the team-building event with the theme of the meeting. For example, I'll choose a strategy theme if we are working on planning or a fun theme if we are celebrating a great quarter. Your father came up with this little piece of wisdom about how to choose the theme based on where the team is "at." He felt there were three Fs of Team Building: Fun, Fast Forward, and Fix. Depending on what the team needed – this helped him guide his choices. I adopted his methodology, and boy, oh boy, does it work! Here is a description of the three Fs to help you along.

Fun: *This is what we have been programmed to believe team building is. It is the traditional times when we get together and get involved in an event or activity that requires us to flex our interpersonal muscles and "get to know each other" while engaging some type of task. This traditionally ranges from a golf trip or celebration dinner to nowadays an escape room or outdoor adventure. No matter which way you slice it, these are amazing opportunities for teams to develop those interpersonal connections in a fun and recreational way (for the most part). These are vital to the development of a team, and are recommended on an as-often-as-possible basis (i.e., time and money budgets).*

Fast Forward: *Here is the most often missed and richest opportunity that managers and leaders have at their disposal. Fast forward is when we integrate team building into the training and daily life of our team. This could mean adding a game structure around a training course and awarding points, badges and winner's circles to promote healthy competition between sales teams with weekly acknowledgements. It could also mean adding a get-to-know-you activity or icebreaker at the beginning of your regular meetings or doing that rewards and recognition stuff you've been putting off. Wise managers seek opportunities within their organization to fit in team functioning into regular training or work life. It's called fast forward because the team collaboration and connectivity improves faster as it is done on a regular basis, not just as a huge annual event.*

Fix: *Sometimes "team" issues become painful. This can be as a result of strained relationships, favouritism, perceptions, downsizing, outsourcing, and the list goes on. Typically, at the core there are some trust issues between your team members, sometimes precipitated by either internal or external issues. Either way, these need to be dealt with so that they don't become caustic and debilitating to your team's progress, connectivity, or profitability. There are many ways to approach "fix" team building, and often they require a consultant, coach, or senior leader's support. These team-building solutions can be very intricate, have long reaches within the business, and take some heavy lifting. Some of the solutions for teams in crisis can include: removing the staff source of contention, group coaching, change of management or employee, or a confrontation event. Any of these solutions require a full toolbox of skills and should not be entered into lightly, or without significant support and planning. All that said, once you "fix" the* *team, you will have opened the way for them to redevelop from a new starting place.*

There you have it. So pick wisely, using all the data you have: MIQ, three Fs, Categories, Intelligences, Equipment, and Time. You got this. I'm proud of you.

GF

(Grandpa — not Gluten Free — LOL)

PS Take care of that rubber chicken.

Let's take a look inside the Rolodex and get this going.

(More in Appendix C – Team Building: Inside the Rolodex of Team Events)

It's not Gambling When You Give Away Poker Chips

This has been one epic day so far. I know when I get a second to breathe I'll be able to process all that has happened with Grandpa. But until I get a few minutes, as he would say, "We have lots of people who need us now."

I glanced down at my watch just as Kim re-entered the office. "Time for my lunch appointment, right?"

"You're getting the hang of this," she said.

"Where are we headed?" I asked.

"Lunch today is in the REC. It was your grandpa's last wish to pass the torch himself to you. So grab a tissue or two if you like. We've got a video to play, his last 'Lunch and Learn' he called it."

Thankfully I got things in place for the team-building event before lunch meeting. Looking over at a painting of my Grandpa on our way to the REC, I say, "I got this…right?"

My phone vibrated in my pocket. Another calendar alert. "Lunch and Learn—you got this." I read it twice. Did he…? Can he…? Was he…? Never mind, I must be tired.

Kim handed me a poker chip and said it was the message of the Lunch and Learn. She reminded me that one of my responsibilities is to start the meeting off with an energizer, something fun that gets people together and warms them up for the upcoming content of the meeting. Because our MIQ fingerprint of the business is largely Interpersonal and Verbal/Linguistic she suggested playing Coffee Talk. Also, it was Grandpa's favourite, so that would be a nice way to start.

I'm not in any position to argue with Kim; she has her fingers firmly placed on the pulse of this place. Coffee Talk it is.

The tone is a bit different from this morning, but not back to the usual ruckus that a Lunch and Learn could be. Without wasting any time I made my way toward the stage. I tried to remind myself of all the things I was taught about running effective icebreakers or energizers because this Lunch and Learn mattered. Jogging my memory, here's what I came up with:

1. MIQ - *Make sure the icebreaker or energizer fits within the Multiple Intelligences of the team you are working with.*

2. Practice - *Make sure you have run the activity before. Try it first with friends or family. It should be well rehearsed so you know it backward and forward.*

3. Fresh - *Make sure you seek out new activities for an existing group. Part of the fun is trying new and innovative things (though sometimes the "fav event of all time" is fun to repeat).*

4. Table Set - *Make sure for a new group you spend some time setting the table for great interaction by getting them to share names and an easy fun fact about themselves. Then build from there.*

5. Energy - *Make sure the energy goes up. The team will feel your enthusiasm as well as the content of the energizer.*

6. Finish - *Make sure to finish the activity when people are having the most fun. Keep the energy mounting, and when you think it has peaked, it's time to bring the activity to a close.*

7. Authenticity - *Make sure you pick activities that represent not only the MIQ of your team but also align with your style and personality as a leader. There is nothing worse than fake cheese—especially canned fake cheese.*

8. Readiness - *Make sure your group is ready for the activity. There are things that aren't easy for everyone to do, so you have to progressively move them toward them if you can, like sharing thoughts, or even shaking hands—some people really hate shaking hands.*

9. Rules - *Make sure you explain the rules of the activity, invite questions for clarification, do a summary of the high points of the guidelines, then go. Walk around to make sure people understand; if they don't, stop early on and re-explain the rules.*

10. Fun - *Make sure you laugh and have fun, too. "Energy is caught not taught," Grandpa always said. Smile so deeply that it radiates from your whole body.*

Reminding myself of these principles, I found that very smile inside my exhaustion. I knew I could rest later. As a leader, it was my job to be mindful and present. Grandpa used to say, "Being present is our greatest gift." I always liked how he said that, even though I had heard it a thousand times before.

I pulled the stage microphone toward my face, and we played Grandpa's favourite game of Coffee Talk. And it was awesome!

(More in Appendix D – Icebreakers: Breaking the Ice and Energizing Your Team)

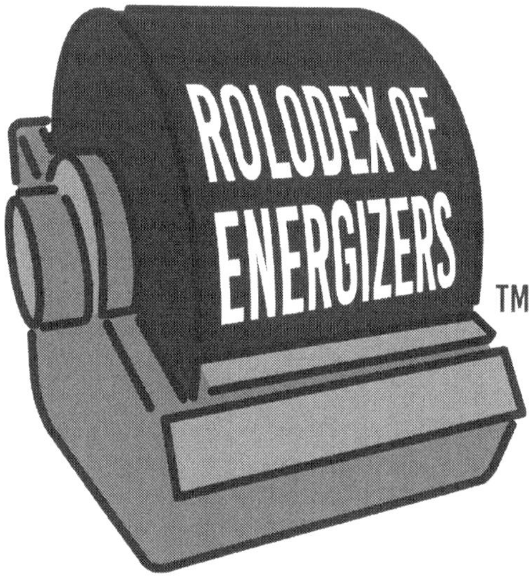
ROLODEX OF
ENERGIZERS
TM

Once the energizer was complete, I was looking out over a room buzzing with the energy I remembered. Smiling faces, beaming with love, and the odd fidgeting employee. It's hard to keep energized employees still and their chatter to a minimum. So I went straight into it.

"Hey everybody, it's been quite a day. I have to say, I have had the opportunity to walk around our offices here and, wow, you totally inspire me. Our business is strong, our people are amazing, and the future is going to be like hitting the jackpot in Vegas." I held up the poker chip. "Today is my grandpa's show; he recorded a message for everyone so I'm going to get Travis to get the tech going. Take it away Travis."

And with that Grandpa graced the spinnaker-sized projection screens.

Well I guess if you're watching this it's my last Lunch and Learn. Thanks so much, Kim, for remembering to get this organized for me

today—you are the best. I wanted to take a moment to tell all of you that you have made such an amazing difference in my life, and the lives of each other. I received an email with a link from my friend Laurie with a link to a YouTube video by a gentleman named Richard Lavoie. He is spectacular. He had a piggy bank filled with poker chips. He said that in life people are either adding poker chips to our piggy bank or taking them away. And we all know that in life we want a full piggy bank as much as possible. We fill each other's piggy banks by demonstrating mutual respect, love, and caring. I want to give each of you a poker chip to remember that important lesson. Our major currency as a team is how we respect each other.

Developing mutual respect in our workplace is similar to filling a piggy bank. As a leader and team member, we should be constantly putting esteem deposits into each other's piggy banks. Be conscious of building a culture here that identifies small positive esteem investments, from appreciations to rewards and compliments to recognition.

As much as we can, try to grow the investment in the piggy bank to overflowing within our team and business. Chances are we will never make it to overflowing (and if we do isn't that a great problem to have), as inevitably a negative event will happen and we will lose some of our esteem investment. The hope is that over time we have invested so much into the piggy bank that we don't become esteem bankrupt and will have something to rebuild from as we continue with more small investments over time.

According to Richard Lavoie, it is essential to build people up with as much investment as possible every day. We need to make sure that people leave their daily experience here with more poker chips in their piggy bank than they came with. To do that, it is important that we take away only what we need from them when there is an issue, and advocate for them when others are trying to take them away.

So, here are some ideas for Building Mutual Respect in the Workplace:

√ *Listen to the concerns of the staff members, take action, and report back.*

√ *Follow through on commitments.*

√ *Listen and inquire so that you have full understanding of what is being said.*

√ *Be frugal in your reprimands; short, accurate, and fair is best.*

√ *Advocate for your team members.*

√ *Conduct yourself with the other person's esteem in mind.*

√ *Build on your positive shared experiences.*

√ *Demonstrate your reliability through your actions.*

√ *Earn respect by sharing opportunities equally.*

√ *Act in a fairly and timely manner to address issues.*

√ *Be open to feedback from others about your performance.*

√ *Actively seek advice and wisdom when making decisions.*

√ *Collaborate on projects wherever possible.*

√ *Share with your team the accolades of a job well done.*

I want to share with each of you your very own poker chip. It is my gift to you for a job well done. You have shown me the love and caring, the dedication and work ethic, and fun and innovation that I could have never imagined. I am truly blessed to have had each of you in my life. And now today I formally ask you to keep being yourselves—and make even more magic in our next chapter as a business with my grandson, John.

With that Travis turned the spotlight toward me. It was my turn. And Grandpa was right, I had this

(More in Appendix E – The Piggy Bank: Rewarding, Recognizing, and Appreciating with Intelligence. There is a Rolodex of Ideas for Rewards, Recognitions, and Appreciations.)

Debriefing: Finding the Value of What's Underneath

I fidgeted with my new poker chip as Kim and I navigated the hallways on what seemed like the milk run, talking to every employee about a poker chip moment that Grandpa had given them. Seems he was that leader who made continuous investments in the piggy banks of his business team as much as he did with us in his family.

As we neared the stairs to my office,… "my office,"—the torch had truly been passed—Kim reminded me that I had a Lessons Learned debrief on the Golf Sierra project in the boardroom at two o'clock. Perfect, I thought. Grandpa's leather sofa was calling my name; maybe I'd get an hour's shut-eye. I thanked Kim again for the great Lunch and Learn and asked her to hold my calls.

Before I could reach the sofa in the privacy of my office, my phone dinged again. I expected a message from Grandpa.

Cancel	**Edit Event**	Done
	Lessons Learned Prep	
	Location	
	All-day	

Sure enough, *Lessons Learned Prep* was what the calendar message said. I would sleep later, I guessed. I clicked through the message and read the notes.

Hey John, this is an important Lessons Learned. It is the final meeting for the completion of the Golf Sierra project. There have been lots of cumulative Lessons Learned for the project along the way. Debriefing effectively is part of what we do here. It should be an energized time, too. Remember when we went to Disney and you dropped your little

Eeyore in the fountain, a member of the Disney team came in and took your doll into the store and "dried" the doll off in the magical hair dryer after Eeyore's bath. But really he got you a new one. The magic doesn't stop there. Just like with team building. If it's to be part of what engages and moves our people forward, our team magic never stops.

In everything we do there is a B-M-E. The Beginning is when we come together, get to know one another, set the stage, establish our goals, vision, and more. The Middle is when we get to work, manage the pieces, collaborate, and pull forward to meet our metrics, re-energize, and support each other. The End is when we close all the loops, collect our learnings, and reapply them to future projects, celebrate each other, and find the depth of learning. I want you to go over to the shelf and find my "debriefing" toy. There are some things there to help you along the way.

I remembered that little Eeyore. We were waiting for the Main Street parade. I was playing by the fountain in the shade—who's kidding who, Florida is hot for Canadians even in their winter—and I don't remember exactly how it all happened but Eeyore got soaked, I bawled. Then out of nowhere this Disney employee dressed in blue pants and blue vest appeared and said, "Oh well, I see Eeyore had a bath. If you don't mind, we have a magical dryer in the back to finish his salon experience." And then within seconds he reappeared with "my" Eeyore all dry and ready for the day.

Grandpa was right. It's really easy to take a step back at different stages of the project. Heck, work gets busy, and life gets busier. That authenticity of message and approach is key for managers regardless of the stage of the project. It is helpful to organize things into B-M-E because, first, the stages give leaders an idea of what should be happening with their team at any given moment. Second, the stages help us to understand how to manage and invest our energy appropriately at a given stage. And third, keeping people engaged is easier when they know there is a completion point. There is nothing more frustrating than projects that just keep going and going. Breaking those "continuous" projects into distinct B-M-Es helps engage our teams and avoids frustration with the "groundhog day" sort of repetition. The debrief is an important tool to help us punctuate that "end in sight." It enables us to learn, grow, and connect.

From the shelf I carefully lifted Grandpa's debrief toy: the little rubber man, the hose and plunger from the shelf. I remembered when Grandpa introduced me to this. One day when he was driving me to school, I was in the back seat and the little guy was positioned in the rear window, behind the back seat.

Grandpa said to me, "Hey, John, see that little plunger attached to the plastic hose? Give it a squeeze." I did, and the squeeze inflated the little guy somehow so that he pulled a moon to the car behind us in the school drop-off loop. It was my buddy Duke's mom. She and Duke lost it, laughing.

Grandpa said, "See, John, debriefing can be fun!" And then we lost it, laughing too.

Beside the debriefing toy, I noticed another Rolodex filled with debriefing ideas; thankfully the same key worked for this one.

Inside I found a note in an envelope taped with more duct tape. Grandpa sure loved duct tape – I think he fancied himself a bit of a MacGyver as much as Indiana Jones. Inside the envelope the note, from Grandpa, said:

Countless leaders struggle to get their teams to participate authentically in discussions. The typical pitfall is in their approach because they do not consider several key components that dictate a group's openness to actively participating in a discussion. Here are some of those components; you will see how truly easy it can be to get your group talking.

First, a person who is included in a discussion is given a sense of ownership over its development and ultimately the resulting solution. When a leader invites the team members to participate and legitimately hear what everyone in the group says, the group will feel more empowered to share their thoughts. To achieve this, a leader actively engages the learners in a process that requires their participation.

Second, leaders should ensure that their processing tools use as many of the eight different intelligences as possible. Howard Gardner originally defined seven (an eight was added later) different intelligences that a person can possess to varying degrees. By using only one technique in a discussion, you alienate many of the "would be" participants and ultimately many "would be" solutions. Effective processing involves leaders planning their approach based on the individual learning styles among the group.

Productivity Processing realizes both of these components. It actively engages the participants on an even playing field while guiding them to legitimately share their thoughts and ideas in a way that is personally rewarding. This process involves the team using a product and then performing an activity with the product to spur authentic dialogue. If Productivity Processing were a math equation it would look like this:

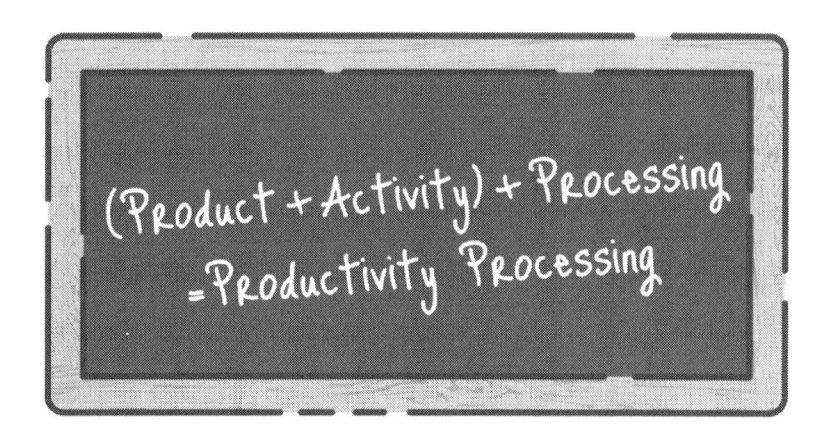

$$(Product + Activity) + Processing = Productivity\ Processing$$

To help you to start using Productivity Processing with your team, let's look at each component of the equation.

1. Product: *The group will create a product that is parallel to the topic under discussion. For example, if you are leading a group of hotel service staff through a process of learning how to improve customer service, you might use a stack of white plates and washable markers to organize problems that staff members identify. The key here is to find a product the participants can comfortably interact with and that will represent clearly the area to be discussed.*

2. Activity: *Once you have a product the group will interact with, it is important to give clear directions for how the product will be used. Continuing with our hotel staff example, the leader would explain, "We are going to write on each plate one problem that is affecting our ability to achieve 100 percent customer satisfaction. The problem could be a specific example or a general topic. Then we are going to organize and stack the plates by topic as represented by the problem that we wrote on the plate." You will give the staff a specific amount of time to yield the product complete the activity. The activity should appeal to as many intelligences as is required or possible. (We will look at these shortly.) Of course, the activity should be enjoyable.*

3. Processing: *Finally, the results of the product and the activity are used to generate dialogue about your specific topic. To commence the processing (and here you can use the Socratic Method, Gestalt, or other techniques), you need to represent the product to the group in a way that summarizes it and inspires thought. In our hotel staff example, stack the dishes one on top of another according to like topics. Doing this will generate a bar graph, which will tell you two things. First, the general areas that need to be discussed, and second, specific examples of problems the staff encounter in customer service. Once you come up with strategies to effectively eliminate the problem, you wash the dish clean. Better yet, leave the dishes with the problems written on them and regularly reconvene the staff to evaluate how they are doing, and clean the plates as problems are resolved.*

4. Productivity Processing: *is a technique that involves everyone in the staff team on an even playing field. As well, it gives you as the leader tangible examples represented in an organized way that can be easily followed up. The purpose of processing with a group is to find a way to illustrate and effectively dialogue about a specific subject and then be able to follow up with a clear action plan to the betterment of your group's objective.*

When you choose Productivity Processing, it is equally important to do it with the best needs of your staff (or client) in mind. Remember, choosing the right mix of product, activity, and processing is important for the group to buy into the process.

That makes sense: we want to build a compelling activity around the debrief if we can. But how do we set up a project so that debriefing becomes part of the life of the venture?

Cancel   **Edit Event**   Done

Look in the dusty book

Location

All-day

With that thought, my phone dinged with another calendar message: *Look in the dusty book.*

Did he…? Was that…? I really needed some sleep! On the very top shelf, I spied a pile of dust with a wave sculpture and a small book underneath it. It was a leadership manual from when Grandpa went to Acadia University. One of the pages was folded over. It read:

Theory of Experiential Education

Many philosophers, educators, psychologists, and researchers have spoken to issues around the role of experience in learning. People like Hahn, Montessori, Piaget, Dewey, and Coleman have all placed value on experience in the learning process.

The general model of Experiential Education as suggested by Kolb (1984) looks like this:

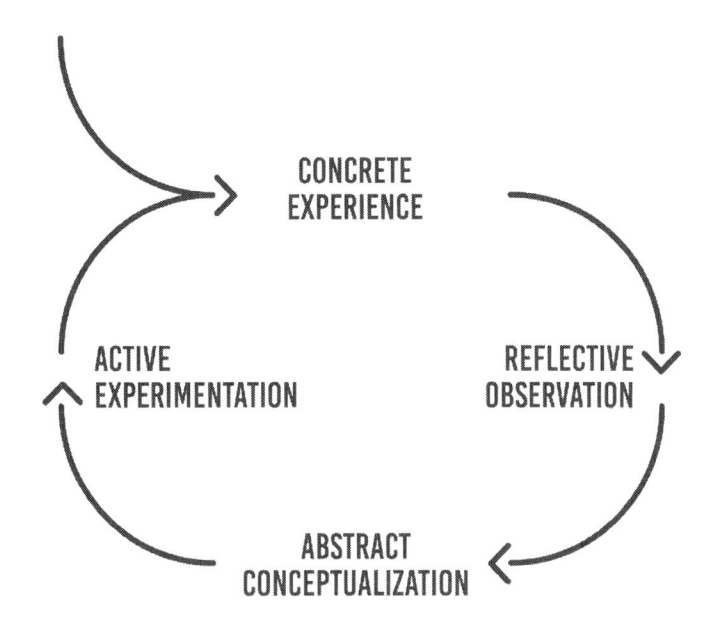

```
        CONCRETE
        EXPERIENCE

ACTIVE                    REFLECTIVE
EXPERIMENTATION           OBSERVATION

        ABSTRACT
        CONCEPTUALIZATION
```

Experiential Learning Cycle

The component parts of Kolb's model can be described as follows:

1. Concrete Experience *is the portion of the model when the learners are actively involved in the physical experience itself. An example of this would be when individuals or a group are climbing a wall, paddling some rapids, playing cards with a senior citizen, or performing a food drive. These various experiences, when appropriately placed, will provide the learners with many opportunities to acquire learning. It is up to the educator to facilitate the learners through the experience so that they maximize their learning outcomes. This is the stage in the cycle where the raw data will be collected by the learners.*

2. Reflective Observation is the segment of the cycle where the learners begin to verbalize what happened in the previous segment. Through active dialogue between members, reflective observation presents unique and collective perspectives among the group. For example, after properly executing a trust sequence, each group member would be able to discuss what they did as a spotter, faller, or spirit spotter and the results experienced. Each perspective would offer a fertile experience of raw data that can be noted through connections of intent and the results of an action or behaviour. Meaning, as a facilitator you are able to help learners create "if" and "then" statements about the experience (i.e., if I catch someone, then I feel successful). This has now created specific connections between what we do and what results.

3. Abstract Conceptualization is the learning segment where the facilitator encourages dialogue around how the learners' reflective observations connect to life. This is the time when learners challenge themselves to think critically about how the resultant stage affected them. For example, when the group made successful catches of each learner in a fall from height they felt successful. In this stage the learners would delve into the idea of success by asking such questions as: why is it important; how do you create it; what is it; etc. By creating a need to replicate this lifestyle function or learning, individuals will seek ways and means of integrating the experience into their everyday lives.

4. Active Experimentation is when learners utilize the learning they have received and implement it in their lifestyle. This involves transferring and acting upon the learning. For example, learners might seek to become more assertive with others or support others more. The learners will act on the learning they received and continue through the learning cycle either through self-direction or follow-up programs.

Adventure Wave

Throughout the Adventure Experience there is an ongoing process of briefing/activity/debriefing. This sequence recurs continuously in a cycle that makes up what is called the Adventure Wave. The waves are professionally sequenced groups of learning experiences that change to meet the immediate and long-term developmental needs of the learners. The Adventure Wave model looks like this:

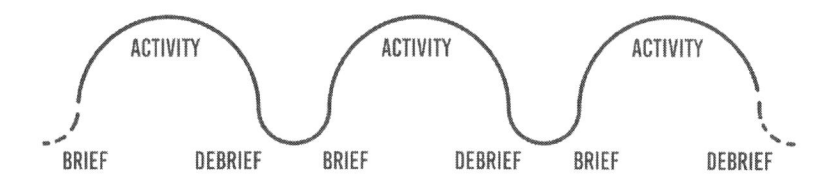

```
   ACTIVITY        ACTIVITY        ACTIVITY
  /        \      /        \      /        \
BRIEF   DEBRIEF BRIEF   DEBRIEF BRIEF   DEBRIEF
```

Adventure Wave

1. *Briefing:* *This area varies in complexity depending on the focus of the group (therapeutic interventions, training and development, recreation, etc.). Essentially, its purpose is to provide the group with the information they require to effectively meet the objectives of the session. In activities done solely for recreational objectives, the facilitator may simply instruct the group in the safety considerations around the session. At the other extreme, the same activity done for therapeutic or training objectives will draw isomorphic connections to a session. In its most basic form this means the facilitator will draw parallel relationships to the outside world with physical things within the session. For example, blindfolds could represent the uncertain future of drug addiction and a rope could serve as the counselling support network available to individuals. The facilitator provides the group with information about what is to come within the activity stage and, in more developed applications, plants seeds for future debriefing. As well, the group will set goals defining how they will function during the session.*

2. *Activity:* *After the briefing comes the activity that you have set for the participants and that they have prepared themselves for. During this part of the Adventure Wave, the participants become actively involved in the episode set before them. The members will express the goals they set out to achieve in the briefing stage through the activity. It is up to the facilitator to monitor the group to ensure that they are respecting the safety requirements and are striving toward the group's and individuals' goals. The facilitator should also be gathering information for the debriefing stage (i.e., making notes).*

3. *Debriefing:* *This has traditionally been the "heady" time of the Adventure Wave. The level of headiness, I believe, is directly proportional to the desired outcomes of the group. For example, a debrief for a recreational activity could be as simple as, "That was fun, wasn't it? Come on over here and let's try this." Debriefing a therapeutic group of trained counsellors and/or psychiatrists, however, could delve into the reasons behind particular behaviours. In the latter example, often isomorphic briefing is used to enhance learning in the debriefing stage. This is because the participants are seeing the connections throughout the experience. For more on this read Michael A. Gass's Book of Metaphors, Volume 2, 1995.*

Although there are many ways of debriefing a group, a structured format includes: What?, So What?, and Now What? This three-tier system enables the facilitator to structure the debrief in a logical sequence, which will aid learners in the transfer of learning from the experience. Here's a simple breakdown of this format:

1. *What?* *This first stage in the structured debrief involves describing what just happened in the activity (simply, it's the play-by-play of the activity). One method I like to use is the VCR—not a real one, a* *fantasy one!* I ask all the members to imagine with me that the activity we just did was recorded on videotape, and I want them to put the tape in the VCR and rewind it. Then I ask one member to explain what they see happening on the TV. In addition, I encourage the rest of the group to feel free to press pause if they think something was missed or if they want to jump in to tell the next part of the story. This VCR method centres the participant through visualization and allows participants to relive the experience by sharing it. Two other methods for the What? stage include: sculpture (participants design a sculpture to describe the activity) and Gestalt (they speak or write in the present tense about the activity; a really good exercise for this method is journal writing).

2. So What? *The second stage of this structured debrief is when you facilitate dialogue around interpreting what the learners derived from the activity. Exploring established group and individual goals often creates an opportunity for fertile dialogue. A quick way to get a general group feeling is to do what is called a "whip." Have each learner finish an open-ended statement with one word. For example, "When I did the fall from height I felt..." This simple exercise will get a general group feeling, which can be used to probe certain feelings, emotions, or learnings. I have found this method of interpreting the experience to be a very successful starting place to encourage fruitful dialogue.*

3. Now What? *This final stage is when the learning is transferred to the next activity and/or real life. The very nature of the Adventure Wave demonstrates the need for learning to be transferred in order to achieve a new learning. That is why the Now What? stage is so important. This is the time when participants will indicate how they will implement the learnings they have received. This is a planning stage when learners decide what they need to do in order to make the things they learned happen in their lifestyles (setting goals, describing what they will do, checking in on each other, etc.).*

Even as a veteran of the experiential learning process, I am constantly searching for the best way to help my group learn from the experiences I put them through. To help you get beyond some of this initial searching, I want to offer you 101 tips for effective facilitation.

1. Get the group in a circle, either sitting knee to knee or standing shoulder to shoulder.

2. Don't leave any unfinished business; terminate all issues appropriately for every learner.

3. Ensure that you maintain eye contact with whoever is speaking.

4. Keep aware of others in the circle: non-verbally acknowledge when it is someone's turn to speak or help focus their attention if they become distracted.

5. Maintain a clear structure, or "rules," for your debrief. A good tool is called the Full Value Contract (the speaker is in charge, respect others and yourself, etc.).

6. Don't be surprised by people's resistance to a debrief; it's often not how learners are used to learning, and it takes some getting used to.

7. Treat what people say with respect.

8. Encourage those who are not participating to speak by asking them direct, fair, and inclusionary questions.

9. Learn from each facilitation session by obtaining evaluation from peers, learners, and yourself.

10. Verbal cues to communicate with them while you're co-facilitating. (Simple ones I have used are leaning forward if I would like to follow a response with a new question direction, and pointing my finger in the air if I have an immediate question).

11. Take discreet notes of the activity and the debrief and refer to them when asking direct questions.

12. One structured format that works for debriefing is Gestalt, which has a questioning format of What?, So What?, and Now What?

13. Sometimes it's best to "let the mountain speak for itself."

14. Be creative and humorous (at appropriate times).

15. Keep notes on each learner so you can have them reflect on things they have already learned or goals they have already set.

16. Take your time, reflect on the learning, and make sure there is a solid awareness among the group about what just happened so they can effectively and efficiently transfer the learning.

17. Ask the tough questions to really challenge your learners.

18. Probe, probe, probe for the deeper meaning within the answer.

19. Read more literature on facilitating a debrief, and understand and apply the theories.

20. Challenge what your learners have said in a developmentally appropriate manner that encourages them to develop their thoughts into meaningful understandings.

21. Choose a key word that a learner has used, and when they have finished their response, simply say the word in an inquisitive manner (i.e., "Respect?" or "Pressure?").

22. Utilize solution-oriented debriefing techniques by asking learners questions about the experience's successes, how learners achieved them, and how the successes can be replicated both directly and indirectly.

23. Support your learners' responses by nodding and being legitimately interested in what they are saying.

24. Use organizers like coloured beads, poker chips, etc., to support accomplishments in different categories.

25. Speak with learners outside the debrief and inquire about how they are, what they've learned, or how they think you are doing.

26. As much as possible, return to the same location to conduct your debrief; learning likes location.

27. Use non-verbal learnings like painting, poetry, or sculpture to support the verbal debrief.

28. Know your audience and speak in a manner in which they will understand, respect, and support you for using.

29. Don't sweat it; do your best.

30. Watch other people facilitate a debrief and borrow techniques you like.

31. Be energized about the learning session (when you're into it, others will get into it).

32. Integrating food into the debrief can be effective as it releases a pleasure chemical in learners' minds (assuming they like what you serve 'em).

33. On the subject of food, snacks or meals are good after intense debriefs—it seems to help relax and re-energize the learners.

34. Practice your speaking techniques in front of groups of people, join the Toastmasters or simply be more active in conversations with strangers while waiting for the bus or having a coffee alone.

35. Write and plan questions that may be helpful during the debrief prior to your session.

36. Take yourself only so seriously; remember to laugh.

37. Attend conferences, and go to sessions on facilitation.

38. Have learners use techniques that involve Creative Visualization (Positive Affirmations, Treasure Mapping, etc.). A good resource for learning how to do this is a book called *Creative Visualization* by Shakti Gawain).

39. Let learners stay connected with the event during the debrief by having them maintain contact with elements of the activity (rope, mouse trap, soft toy, etc.).

40. Conduct a debrief with your learners blindfolded.

41. Try something new when you debrief.

42. Define and plan your outcomes beforehand as recreational, educational, developmental, or therapeutic, and structure the debrief accordingly.

43. Practice your questioning techniques on people you meet—friends, family, roommates, etc. It will help you hone your skills.

44. Set goals for yourself and your debriefing ability.

45. Take the time to pet a friendly dog or cat on the street (OK, maybe it won't help your facilitation skills, but dogs and cats are generally nice creatures).

46. Read or experience things that are appropriate to the learning sessions you provide like research studies on customer relationships, leadership, etc.

47. Speak clearly when you ask questions and provide clarification and connections using examples from the experience and from real life.

48. Create a journal for your learners that speaks to the expected outcomes for each experience.

49. Take photos and collect non-private writings during the sessions and send them to your learners post-experience as a yearbook or family album.

50. Limit external noise that may affect your experience by locating away from major traffic areas, loud machinery, other groups, etc., while remaining as close as possible to the activity site.

51. Make sure you speak authentically.

52. Keep an open and inviting posture toward your learners by not crossing your arms or legs and avoiding adverse facial expressions, etc.

53. Smile.

54. Carry a water bottle and drink from it.

55. Try out the Socratic Method of debriefing (a great explanation of that can be found on pages 152–153 in *Effective Leadership in Adventure Programming* by Simon Priest and Michael Gass).

56. Teach others how to create more effective debriefs by evaluating each other.

57. Ensure that your location has good ventilation.

58. Make sure that there is adequate lighting for the debrief. Lighting can create mood so use things like candles, campfires, and lanterns (the high beams of a car should be used only for interrogations by the FBI).

59. Send you learners a letter that will guide them to dress appropriately, to ensure their comfort during the activity and debrief session (e.g., some clothes are not necessarily conducive to sitting on the floor for a debrief).

60. Get enough rest prior to your session. It helps you become a more effective learning facilitator by helping you energetically think on your feet.

61. Know where to refer people for more specialized information or support, as you might not necessarily be the most qualified person to continue with a debrief. Simply know your limitations, qualifications, and what external resources are available.

62. Co-facilitate with professionals (counsellors, doctors, etc.), especially when there is the potential for the need to administer psychological or medical first aid.

63. Read, understand, and commit to being an ethical experiential educator, a good resource for this is *Ethics in Experiential Education* by J. Hunt.

64. Become aware of people's non-verbal reactions to dialogue; they will speak volumes to a leader who is aware.

65. Respect yourself by knowing your limitations.

66. Know the policies and procedures of the organization that you are working for and how they affect your role as facilitator.

67. Know your employer's or your own ability to insure any legal ramifications that may result from allegations and outcomes of your debrief.

68. Create opportunities for your learners to continue to learn from the experience even post-debrief (i.e., utilize isomorphic connections during the dialogue of the debrief).

69. In all your dealings with your learners, ensure that you create a feeling of trust and respect.

70. Let people talk, don't tell them they're wrong, just keep the dialogue running until you get the learning piece that you want to probe.

71. Role model the positive behaviours outside of your group that you desire from them.

72. Eat gummy bears.

73. Design and use facilities that are learner focused. The learners' comfort is more important than your own (i.e., off-site to reduce interruptions.)

74. Celebrate successful debriefs by sharing effective tools with learners.

75. Finish your debrief as timely as possible. I read once that debriefing was like cheese—too much processing makes Velveeta, so be cognizant of over-and under processing.

76. With some high-functioning groups you will find that after a while they begin to facilitate their own dialogue. Stay interested and help shape the debrief to match your planned learning outcomes.

77. Sometimes it helps at the end of a session to summarize and clarify what was said and learned through the debrief. This can be done by you, one of the learners, or the entire group collectively.

78. Be aware of your voice tone, it affects the learners' energy.

79. Use people's names whenever you can.

80. When you're outside, debrief in shaded areas as the sun can draw energy and be tough on the eyes of some learners.

81. When you're outside, make sure that you, not your learners, are looking into the sun whenever possible.

82. Break groups into solos, dyads, and small and large groups for reflection on learning.

83. Jot down notes while learners are talking through a debrief to remember important points and structure your questioning.

84. When you're outside, take off your sunglasses because "the eyes are the window to the soul."

85. Keep groups to a maximum of fifteen learners whenever possible.

86. Send learners a letter post-program to thank them and support them on their personal pursuits of learning.

87. Be aware of teachable moments and maximize their potential by stopping to investigate the learning when the moment presents itself.

88. Evaluate your program against the objectives you set for the session: do this individually, and invite your learners and colleagues to do the same.

89. Hold a reunion with program learners.

90. As a thumbnail guide, schedule your dialoguing sessions to be as long as you're doing sessions—but remember don't over- or under process the experience.

91. Know your contracting agent's, professional associations, or group's position on confidentiality and adhere to these standards; some groups require you to sign off on a confidentiality clause in your contract.

92. Drink fancy coffees in your free time…just 'cause it's fun!

93. If you don't have time for the debrief post-experience, provide the group with a summary and make time to debrief later, informing the group of this plan.

94. Create an atmosphere that encourages learners to contribute their questions to the dialogue as well as responses to your questions.

95. Choose to engage in regular dialogues with your learners at established times and locations (campfires, after meals, etc.).

96. Quickly gain group consensus using scales of 0 to 10, thumbs up or down, etc.

97. Teach learners to perform relaxation exercises to centre themselves prior to a debrief (i.e., have the group breathe in through the nose for four seconds, hold their breath for seven seconds, and push the air out with the tip of the tongue pressed against the back of the front teeth for eight seconds).

98. Present an open-ended statement that learners can complete like, "Right now I am feeling…" or "My parents are…"

99. Break into dyads and have learners paraphrase and report their partner's responses to questions you provide (this is great when you are short on time).

100. Have learners write down their responses prior to speaking, it helps to collect their thoughts and reduce anxiety about speaking.

101. Have fun.

There was a knock on the office door. Kim was standing there with Gerry, our project lead on the Golf Sierra project. Always a beaming smile on that guy. He laughed when he saw me with the debriefing toy in my hand.

"Hate to cancel your bonding time with the 'debriefer,' but we have a meeting to go to."

I laughed, too, placing the debriefing toy next to the Rolodex of Debriefing and the ocean wave. "Can't wait to see what you have in store for our Productivity Processing Lessons Learned Debrief."

(More in Appendix F – Debriefing: Learning with Intelligence.)

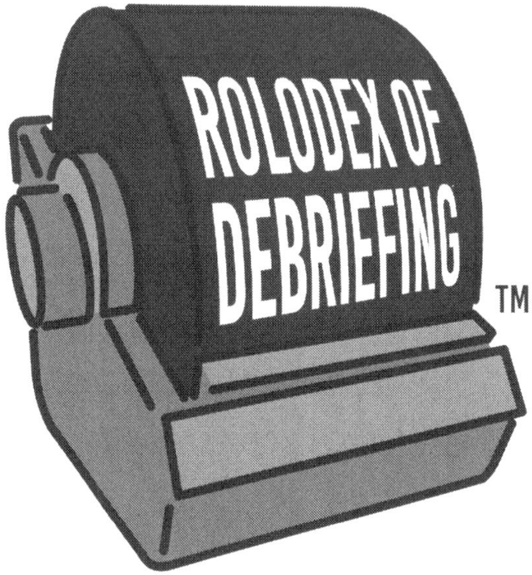
ROLODEX OF
DEBRIEFING
TM

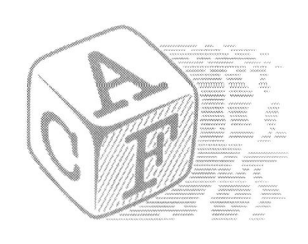

Inside the Brain Sculpture:
Multiple Intelligences of Teams

Interpersonal Learner (The "People" Learner)

This intelligence indicates a keen ability to relate to and understand others. These learners have a seemingly innate ability to see things from other people's perspectives in order to understand how they think and feel. They often have an uncanny ability to sense the feelings, intentions, and motivations of others.

They are great organizers, although they sometimes resort to manipulation to achieve their ends. Generally, they encourage group peace and cooperation. They use both verbal and non-verbal language to open communication channels with others. (Examples of these learners: counsellor, salesperson, businessperson, clergy, service personnel.)

Modalities of Interpersonal Learners

- Easily build rapport with others.
- Easily make friends with co-workers.
- Find commonalities with others.
- The first to reach out to new workers or workers in distress.
- Sense feelings in others (and can manipulate those feelings).
- Streetwise and confident.
- Read a group's feelings in meetings, events, etc.
- Use people's feelings to meet their ends, or what they feel are the best ends for the group.

Master communicators both verbally and non-verbally.

- Typically speak well with others in large and small groups.
- Will match energy of the people they are working with, becoming the "social chameleon."
- Passionate speakers who empower others by "pushing the right buttons."

Great organizers and collaborators.

- First to step up and lead an event or initiative.
- Want to have "help" from others for anything they are doing.
- Check in with others as discussion happens and makes sure everyone is on-board for the solution.
- Like to feel like they are part of something bigger

How to Lead and Manage with Intelligence Energizing

- Give public recognition for a job well done.
- Provide them with work assignments that involve others, and ask them to lead the initiative.

Communicating

- A face-to-face discussion is best for this worker.
- Conflict-based discussions are best done in private.
- Will ensure that all are heard in a group setting.
- Will typically side with the group.

- Let them know how you feel about what you are shaing.

Building Trust

- Keep the best interests of the group in mind.
- Be fair, consistent, and authentic toward others.
- Empower them to take a lead in projects and coach them to success.

Teaching/Coaching

- They will learn best in a group setting.
- Retreats, meetings, etc., work well for these learners.
- Read their non-verbal and verbal cues, as they want to tell you exactly how they are feeling/
- what they are thinking.

Leading/Managing

- Give them the opportunity to lead projects and pieces of projects.
- Ensure that they are with others for their jobs.
- Utilize their social influence to advance your project needs.

Managing with Intelligence To Dos

- Be conscious of your body language.
- Encourage discussion.
- Have them present to other employees.

- Provide personal feedback.
- Have them mentor others and be mentored.
- Allow them to plan group activities.
- Address how people's emotions have been impacted.
- Beware of their strong ability to manipulate a situation to achieve their desires.
- Great organizers for events and initiatives.
- Watch for both verbal and non-verbal body language cues of what they are thinking.

We like to:

- Care for others.
- Show feelings through body language.
- Coach/counsel others.
- Have human contact.

We are good at:

- Communicating with others.
- Cooperation.
- Teamwork.
- Interpreting social cues.
- Manipulating others.

Intrapersonal Learner (The "Thinker" Learner)

This intelligence indicates a keen awareness of one's inner state of being. These learners try to understand their inner feelings, dreams, relationships with others, and strengths and weaknesses. (Examples of these learners: researcher, adventurer, explorer, philosopher.)

Modalities of Intrapersonal Learners

- Like to think about and envision the solution.
- Important to have alignment with vision and mission.
- Explore visioning statements and explore cause and effects of actions taken.

Enjoy researching and fact finding.

- Find information before the project starts and ensure facts are correct.
- Lurk on the internet, seeking benchmark solutions by other organizations.
- Will "call" you on your facts or question for clarification about what you say.

Enjoy working in a solitary environment.

- Find open office situations difficult, hence like their own "cave" to work in.
- Know that working in a group is often required, but prefer to have a job that feeds
- information back to the group.

Internally driven, based on their values and beliefs.

- Passionate workers when their values and beliefs are aligned with the vision/mission of
- the project.
- Self-motivated, self-critical, and self-rewarded for the most part.

How to Lead and Manage with Intelligence

- Energizing
- Keep the accolades private and meaningful.
- Keep their work assignment attached to things they value and believe in.
- Reward them with something that demonstrates you understand them.

Communicating

- Connect in ways that allow them time to consider and craft a response, i.e., email.
- Craft the message to attach to their value centres to in spire them to take charge.

Building Trust

- Consider their need for privacy and time to reflect on information.
- Asking them to take a leap of faith is not something they are comfortable with.

Teaching/Coaching

- Provide them with assignments and projects that require them to self-discover the information.
- Smaller group settings are more comfortable.
- Conversation will happen in short spurts, unless they are passionate about the topic.

Leading/Managing

- Enjoy the mentor/mentee relationship.
- As a manager they tend to be cut and dry about decision-making; you may have to soften
- their actions.
- Touch base with them one-to-one to get full details.

Managing with Intelligence To Dos

- Use email to correspond.
- Give them a task and allow them to research the best way, for them, to carry it out.
- Involve them in the visioning part of the business/task.
- Encourage self-reflection after a task.
- Connect how their role connects to others.
- Internally motivated by how what they are doing makes them feel.

- These employees will understand their weaknesses and strengths very well, but may not let
- you know and harbour how they feel about their performance.

We like to:

- Work on our own goals.
- Consider our own strengths and weaknesses.
- Think.
- Self-reflect.
- Self-discover.

We are good at:

- Isolated tasks.
- Self-evaluation.
- Thinking critically.
- Visioning.
- Internal motivation.

Bodily/Kinesthetic (The "Doer" Learner)

This intelligence indicates a well-developed sense of body control and movement while being able to handle objects skillfully. These learners express themselves well through movement. By interacting with the space around them, they are able to remember and process information. (Examples of these learners: athlete, firefighter, coach, police, dancer, actor.)

Modalities of Bodily/Kinesthetic

- Great fine and gross motor skills.
- Handle objects skillfully, clear sense of "goal" with a physical action.
- Able to train physical responses.
- Willing to "chip in and help."

Speaks with Body Language.

- Express feelings through body language.
- Can explain things using gestures.
- Often uses touch to communicate ideas or appreciation.

Shorter attention span.

- Follow short explanations.
- Not fans of sitting still for long periods of time.
- Often considered hyperactive.
- Need frequent short breaks.

Memory is movement.

- Will try and try again physical ways of solving a problem.
- Memory is improved when physical action is required to solve an issue.

How to Lead and Manage with Intelligence

- Energizing
- Provide quick physical contact (e.g., high five, hand shake).
- Give them time, support, and opportunity to explore solutions.

Communicating

- Keep explanations short.
- Use demonstrations and props for examples.
- Set physical and time goals for projects.
- Don't set a lot of reading time.

Building Trust

- Don't lecture them and encourage them to "do."
- Give them jobs that see them in front of the group, building solutions and achieving goals
- that can be physically measured.
- Respect leaders who achieve goals.

Teaching/Coaching

- Practice the task together.
- Role play situations.
- Use props and other tangibles.
- Involve them in on-the-job training.
- Involve building/constructing/doing as much as possible.

Leading/Managing

- Be face-to-face as often as possible.
- Champion their active solution finding.
- Keep employees moving and doing.
- Be efficient with your words.
- Let them "do."

Managing with Intelligence To Dos

- Use props or tangibles during explanation.
- Keep explanations very short.
- Connect to everyday life activities.
- Have them build models/displays.
- On-the-job training.
- Practice the task.
- Role play solutions.
- Use visualization to describe or learn things.

- Watch their body for cues as to how they feel and what they think.

We like to:

- Coach others.
- Assess workplace ergonomics.
- Take a tactile approach to tasks.
- Move while we work.
- Demonstrate tasks.

We are good at:

- Manual dexterity.
- Agility, balance.
- Hand-eye coordination.
- Bodily expression of ideas.
- Making things.
- Strength.
- Speed.
- Flexibility.

Verbal/Linguistic Learner (The "Word" Learner)

This intelligence indicates a highly developed ability to use words and language effectively. Individuals have highly developed auditory skills and generally are very good speakers. Learners with a heightened Linguistic Intelligence tend to think in terms of words rather than pictures. (Examples of these learners: lawyer, teacher, sales, consultant, politician.)

Modalities of Verbal/Linguistic Learner

- Strong acuity for the written word.
- Excellent readers and decoders of information.
- Can distill and represent information to your group in a way that all can understand.
- Prepare written copy very well.

Strong ability in using the spoken word.

- Able to organize presentation data to groups in an interesting and well-thought-out manner.
- Comfortable orators and present well.
- Often repeat what is heard to clarify.

Use humour and irony well.

- Deftly use words to present ideas, and does so in an entertaining way.
- Quick-witted and easily make links to ideas and present them back to their audience.

Great listeners.

- Very comfortable listening to others; seek to understand and will seek clarification until they do.

- Keen ability to discern nuances of what people mean (which may differ from what they are saying) when they are speaking.

How to Lead and Manage with Intelligence

- Energizing

- Encourage them to make presentations on behalf of the group.

- Tell them a story about how something they did really mattered and made a difference.

Communicating

- Employees like to take notes and clarify what was said.

- Excellent at written and spoken communication tools.

- Supportive for editing and double-checking work.

- Enjoys a good debate.

Building Trust

- Ensure that your data is accurate and presented well.

- Take time to connect and tell stories together.

- Listen to what they have to say; don't cut them off.

Teaching/Coaching

- Provide documentation that they can refer to.
- Presented in verbal or written format for best retention.
- Let them explain to you what they learned/know.

Leading/Managing

- Consult with them to find solutions.
- They will argue/debate with you about the appropriate solutions or approaches.
- They have an opinion, and it matters a lot to them.

Managing with Intelligence To Dos

- Present task verbally.
- Ask questions of employees to clarify explanations.
- Use words not visuals to explain.
- Ask employees to put together policy/handbooks.
- Can present materials very well verbally.
- Storytelling will be important in your discussions with these employees.
- Humour/irony are strengths with these employees.

We like to:

- Write policy procedure.
- Edit copy.

- Prepare a speech.
- Spin a story to the positive or negative.
- Write instructions.

We are good at:

- Commentating on an event.
- Writing.
- Editing.
- Reaching people with language.
- Humour.
- Irony.

Visual/Spatial Learner (The "Visual" Learner)

This intelligence indicates an increased ability to perceive the visual cues. Individuals tend to think in terms of pictures and movies. In order to retain information, they need to create vivid visual images. (Examples of these learners: artist, mechanic, web/graphic designer, architect.)

Modalities of Visual/Spatial Learner

- Visually perceive the spatial world accurately.

- Able to view and interpret what's happening (like a hunter or guide reading the trails or wilderness) and assimilate the pieces to form an understanding.

Transform their understanding into a physical representation.

- Able to express their understanding of their world around them through a visual image (e.g., painting, drawing, sculpture, photograph).

- Able to graphically represent a concept for others to understand. *Sensitive to shape, colour, line, space, etc., and how they interrelate.*

- Aware of how shapes, colour, etc., connect and complement or detract from each other. This is how an interior designer, for example, can take your same furniture and arrange it to make it more appealing.

How to Lead and Manage with Intelligence

- Energizing
- Involve them in projects where they can construct, draw, layout, video, etc.

Communicating

- Speak in terms of how they see the final product or process.
- Have a visual that represents your message where posible.

Building Trust

- Find ways of appreciating the "beauty or form" of what they have laid out within their work.
- Ask them questions about their work and why they made it.

Teaching/Coaching

- Encourage visualization of the end results or thing to learn.
- Provide a handout for after the learning event.
- Empower employees to build their own visual of the learning.

Leading/Managing

- Install visual reminders at workstations.
- Use visual supports wherever possible, i.e., maps, charts, diagrams.

Managing with Intelligence To Dos

- Use visuals such as charts, maps, or movies to illustrate explanations.

- Ask employees to design displays/marketing visuals.
- Use timelines and concept mapping to tie tasks together.
- Provide employees with documentation/handout to support verbal explanation.
- Create connections with analogies and metaphors when explaining concepts or effects of actions.

We like to:

- Create room layouts/logos/presentations/etc.
- Pack equipment or the car.
- Create costumes/displays/etc.
- Draw diagrams.
- Build examples.

We are good at:

- Organizing a 3D space.
- Making things look good.
- Decorating.
- Building "curb appeal."
- Simplifying lots of items into a defined space.

Logical/Mathematical Learner (The "Numbers" Learner)

This intelligence indicates a heightened ability to use reason, logic, and numbers effectively. These learners think conceptually in logical and numerical patterns, making connections between pieces of information. They are very curious about the world around them. They ask a lot of questions and enjoy experimenting. (Examples of these learners: medical personnel, accountant, scientist, researcher, engineer.)

Modalities of Logical/Mathematical Learners

- Keen number sense.
- An unparalleled ability to manipulate, understand, and use numbers.
- They like things explained in concrete terms, category, classification, calculation, etc.

Ability to reason well.

- Able to connect pieces of data to make sense of a problem.
- Able to think logically, and often without emotion, about what the correct answer is, and
- unless there is new data, this will be the only option.

Strong sense of logical patterns/relationships an statements/propositions.

- Think in terms of "cause-effect" and "if-then."
- A clear path is important for most regular task requests, or be clear that they are "

- problem-solving" and you want their solution.

Ability to think abstractly.

- Will build and test hypotheses.
- Will take existing data and solve for x by generalizing and making inferences.

How to Lead and Manage with Intelligence

- Energizing
- Challenge them to find answers.
- Let them experiment to find better ways of doing things or better answers.

Communicating

- Keep explanations short.
- Ensure that you have metrics in what you are trying to get across.
- Give them time to ask questions; don't fluff the answer, or they will call you on it.

Building Trust

- Follow through on what you say.
- Solicit their opinion, and act on their information.

Teaching/Coaching

- Ensure that you can demonstrate cause and effect or if and then to these learners.

- Keep things short, sweet, and to the point.
- Ensure that you can measure what you are doing or demonstrating.
- Use a brain teaser to get their attention.

Leading/Managing

- Manage by the numbers.
- Keep your explanations logical, short, and measured.
- Show logical sequence to things to gain buy-in.

Managing with Intelligence To Dos

- Short explanations.
- Use numbers/figures to clarify or justify initiatives.
- Give step-by-step instruction.
- Use a brain teaser to get their attention.
- Make the logical connection.
- Be able to adequately answer the "whys".
- Do not get frustrated by questions because they will have lots of them.
- Encourage their active experimentation toward finding solutions.
- Challenge them to search for the answers.

We like to:

- Troubleshoot.

- Solve problems.
- Negotiate and make deals
- Build a strategy.
- Assess value.
- Measure something difficult.
- Valuate something.

We are good at:
- Numbers
- Logic.
- Analyzing problems.
- Setting logical paths.
- Making/testing hypotheses.
- Classifying and categorizing.

Musical Learner (The "Music" Learner)

This intelligence indicates an increased ability to produce and appreciate anything musical. Individuals tend to think in terms of sounds, rhythms, and patterns. They are affected deeply by what they hear and can become distracted by external noise. (Examples of these learners: DJ, musician, composer, singer, etc.)

Modalities of Musical Learners

- Sound and rhythm move them.
- A properly placed sound bite or song can inspire and hook this person.
- Connecting actions to an alliteration or rhythmic sounding term will connect with this person
- (i.e. screw down so you don't screw up)

Thinks in terms of patterns.

- This employee will see how events and episodes happen in rhythm or pattern, can help
- with planning and problem identification.
- Often build a good tempo for working with repetitive jobs.
- Interested in finding logical patterns to work (opposite drives them crazy).

Easily distracted by external noise.

- This employee needs to have a space that has logical noise (random, external noises

- distract - music or rhythmic noise inspires).
- Let them choose the music by which they work.

Able to perceive, discriminate, transform and perform.

- He or she can deconstruct a piece of music either from a technical or intuitive standpoint. They can understand create & perform music.

How to Lead and Manage with Intelligence

- Energizing
- Inspired by music. Allowing them to listen to music while performing appropriate work tasks
- is welcomed.
- Invest their skills in tasks with flow and pattern.

Communicating

- Ensure that your room is clear from external random noises.
- Share things in terms of "how they sound" i.e. "boom"

Building Trust

- Be sensitive to their needs and don't push too hard, they can be critical of themselves until
- they are satisfied with what they have built... & satisfaction takes time.

Teaching/Coaching

- Connect learning to a theme inspired by a piece of music.

- Inspire them to help deconstruct or construct the pattern required to "achieve" something.
- Develop lingoes and catchy rhymes to solidify learning.

Leading/Managing

- Set up logical patterns and sequences where possible.
- They have a tendency to not be "excited" about end product until it is perfect… but don't
- wait for it, it often never comes.

Managing with Intelligence To Dos

- Attempt to demonstrate a pattern.
- Allow music to play in the background of their work environment, if appropriate.
- Have them develop lingoes, catchy rhymes to demonstrate an important staff guideline.
- Set up logical sequences of events and flow in the workplace.
- Explain things in terms of how they would sound.

We like to:

- Play and listen to music.
- Make catchy rhymes to remember things.
- Set music to play for an event (i.e. phone hold/lobby).
- Teach someone to play music.

We are good at:

- Finding rhythms and patterns.
- Mimicking sounds.
- Reviewing musical work.
- Coaching vocal/speaking performances.

Naturalist Learner (The "Nature" Learner)

This intelligence indicates a keen ability to see the connections and cycles of natural processes. These learners enjoy classifying things into areas of responsibility, placement, and category. They easily connect cause and effect and illustrate patterns. They appreciate knowing how things are connected to real life. (Examples of these learners: project manager, landscaper, outdoor guide, engineer, etc.)

Modalities of Naturalist Learner

- Expert at recognition and classification.
- Readily recognize and classify flora and fauna (or if raised in an urban setting, "things" such
- as cars, sneakers, etc.).
- Handily categorize based on a set of rules or under-standings.

Sensitive to systems that happen around them.

- Aware of other systems around them (e.g., flow of energy, water cycle). By understanding
- these systems they apply that natural flow to other facets of their lives.

Understand natural cause and effect.

- Know that there are natural consequences to all of our actions. They are accepting of logical
- cause and effect, applied to real life.

Able to express a macro view of flow and processes.

- Have an unparalleled ability to present a 30,000-foot view of how a process should work.
- Understand innately how things connect together, how smaller actions can be classified, and
- how to deliver a path/flow of that info.

How to Lead and Manage with Intelligence

- Energizing
- Bring natural things into the office space, such as water features, plants, etc., or take them
- outside for meetings.
- Show social responsibility toward the environment.

Communicating

- Connect your message to real life.
- Talk in terms of process and flow.

Building Trust

- Ensure that your actions run in partnership with how the natural world works (i.e., concern
- for the environment, concern for community).

Teaching/Coaching

- Draw natural connections to the things you are talking about or what you are asking

- these employees to do.
- Classify things into logical chunks, such as areas of responsibility, time to perform, etc.
- Have them do site visits to understand how things connect and work.

Leading/Managing

- Provide maps, charts, and simulations to explain and guide performance.
- Engage employees in building systems and logical flow.

Managing with Intelligence To Dos

- Attempt to use analogies of nature (systems in work flow).
- Relate business cycles and interconnectedness to cycles in nature.
- Illustrate patterns in explanations of how to do things.
- Connect tasks to real life.
- Demonstrate cause and effect.
- Classify things into areas of responsibility, placement, etc.

We like to:

- Be with nature.
- Understand cause and effect.
- See flow/cycles/interconnectedness of things.

- Define categories.
- Build processes.

We are good at:
- Categorizing.
- Discriminating between things.
- Connecting the big-picture items.
- Being sensitive to the environment.

Online Tools:
Multiple Intelligences Quotient

Team Building with Intelligence: MIQ Self-Test

Rate the following statements according to the scale below

(5 = I'm always like that, to 1 = I'm never like that) in the blank column. The higher the numbers on your score card below the greater the intelligence in that area.

5 = I'm always like that.

4 = I'm often like that.

3 = I'm sometimes like that.

2 = I'm rarely like that.

1 = I'm never like that.

1	I love to move around while I work.
2	I get easily distracted by external noise.
3	I easily see things from other people's perspectives.
4	I am keenly aware of my personal strengths and weaknesses.
5	I love to write with a computer or by hand, on paper.
6	I like to do logic puzzles and brainteasers.

7	I am keenly interested in caring for the planet and actively recycle, compost, etc.
8	I like to explain and learn things using diagrams, maps, or illustrations.
9	I like to make my decisions based on numbers.
10	I like to daydream.
11	I like to decorate and design rooms.
12	I can easily find the irony or humour in situations.
13	I like to categorize and discriminate among things based on their characteristics.
14	I learn the tasks of the job best by doing them.
15	I can make music by playing instruments like piano, guitar, etc.
16	I love being a mentor, and being mentored.
17	I love telling jokes and stories.
18	I love a catchy rhyme or jingle to help remember things.
19	I love to play sports and be physically active.
20	I love to problem-solve and troubleshoot.
21	I easily understand the cause and effect of things.
22	I often think in terms of movies and pictures.
23	I like to make sure that everyone is heard in a group discussion.

24	I enjoy the visioning part of business/tasks.
25	I like spending time in nature, i.e., gardening, camping, birdwatching.
26	I like to draw and doodle.
27	I love to make a playlist of music that expresses how I'm feeling.
28	I love to spend time reading books and magazines.
29	I enjoy analyzing and measuring things.
30	I love planning group activities.
31	I get fidgety if I sit for too long.
32	I like to research the best ways to do things before taking action.
33	I enjoy making things, i.e., construction, models, cooking.
34	I make new friends easily.
35	I like to write down instructions, and I'm really good at it.
36	I like a strategy toward accomplishing things.
37	I like spending time by myself.
38	I can "hear" what people are saying by the tone of their voice.
39	I love to build processes to get things done.
40	I can see how to pack equipment or a car so everything fits perfectly.

MIQ – Score Card

Add up the value you gave for all the questions. Place your total score in the third column, below. Then plot your answers on the MIQ Fingerprint graphic.

	1, 14, 19, 31, 33	
	2, 15, 18, 27, 38	
	3, 16, 23, 30, 34	
	4, 10, 24, 32, 37	
	6, 9, 20, 29, 36	
	7, 13, 21, 25, 39	
	8, 11, 22, 26, 40	
	5, 12, 17, 28, 35	

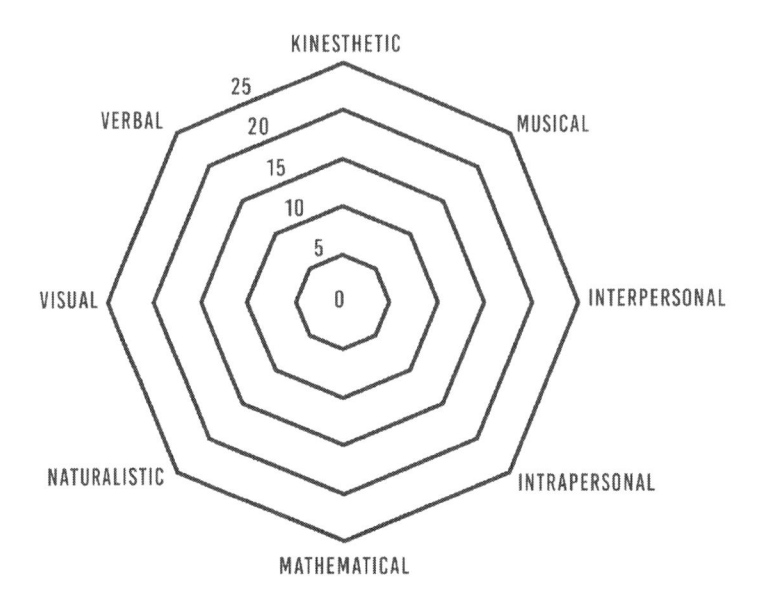

Visit: www.teambuildingactivities.com/MIQtool for downloads and other useful tools.

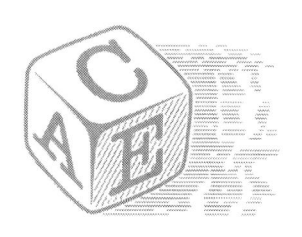

Team Building: Inside the Rolodex of Team Events

ROLODEX OF DEBRIEFING™

ROLODEX OF REWARDS™

ROLODEX OF ENERGIZERS™

1. PASSION

Passion is energy. Feel the power that comes from focusing on what excites you.

Oprah Winfrey

Yes, in all my research, the greatest leaders looked inward and were able to tell a good story with authenticity and passion.

Deepak Chopra

The secret of passion is purpose.

Robin Sharma

The first part of creating engagement within our teams is getting to know the people you work with. *Rah-rah* in your staff is not what team engagement is. Team engagement comes from an individual employee's passion about their work beyond their pay cheque. It is a manager's job to discover, acknowledge, and encourage an employee's passion. Through the conscious caring and nurturing of passion, you can transform a workplace into an engaged culture.

With each activity, think about what your team members are passionate about. That passion is the touchpoint that will help you to deepen their engagement—inspire them—and motivate them go beyond the work to get a pay cheque.

PASSION INVENTORY

Intelligences: Intrapersonal, Logical/Mathematical, Naturalist

Time: 30 min

You need: spreadsheet

Sit and assess what each of your team members is passionate about. Print a table with the employees' names listed in column A. Then, in the other columns brainstorm passion points/examples related to the following topics for each employee. Use those passion points to motivate, distribute tasks, encourage, etc., your team members.

- Task at which they regularly surpass expectations
- Subject outside of work they always talk about
- Reason why they took this job
- Things team members compliment them on

FIREWALL

Intelligences: Interpersonal, Bodily/Kinesthetic, Visual/Spatial

Time: 20 min

You need: Pen/pencil, paper, tape

At the end of the day, host a 10-minute team meeting. Have each employee write the thing that they are most passionate about in their work. Take ten seconds per employee and have them tell the team what this thing is and then post it up on the firewall (a designated spot—you can decorate it if you want). This way, folks can share their passion, talk about what's happening at work, and fill your inventory with data of individual passions.

BRAND OF US

Intelligences: Verbal/Linguistic, Visual/Spatial, Interpersonal

Time: 30 min to 2 hr

You need: Whiteboard, markers

A truly successful team has a brand that is easily understood by the team members and by those looking in. As a leader, helping your team to understand and live that brand will encourage engagement and passion in the work employees do. Here is a simple activity your can do that can feed future actions (i.e., reward branding, logo design, communication styles, etc.) by creating clarity of team brand. The output from this exercise will tell you how to engage with stakeholders so that you are providing a clear message.

Draw your team together (three to twenty people). In the centre of your whiteboard draw a circle and inside the circle define who your team is: mission/vision kind of stuff. From there draw a line and a circle that connects to your centre circle. In that circle name one of the stakeholders or influencers on your team (i.e., customers, senior management, suppliers, etc.). Ask, "What does this group need to experience from us to support us?" Encourage your team to think in 30,000-foot view terms not the minutia of the connections. Once you have explored your various stakeholders/influencers, look for common brand descriptors (e.g., fun, trustworthy, attention to detail). Post these words around your office, ensure external/internal communications reflect this brand, invest in your work with these brand characteristics, and coach your team to ensure that everyone is delivering a consistent message.

LOTTERY WIN

Intelligences: Bodily/Kinesthetic, Naturalist, Logical/Mathematical

Time: 20 min

You need: Fake cheques, pens/pencils

Host a 15-minute meeting with your team. Make up a fake cheque for each of your employees for $10 million. Inform your team that they have just won the lottery. But instead of keeping the money for themselves they have to donate it to a group(s) that do important work for things in the world they are passionate about (e.g., cleaning up the oceans, building schools, eliminating hunger, etc.). Have them write on the back of the cheque the amount of their winning they would allocate to each group, or all of it to one group.

WHY HERE? WHY THIS?

Intelligences: Interpersonal, Verbal/Linguistic, Logical/Mathematical

Time: 20 min

You need: Nothing specific required for this activity

This is a great conversation to have at onboarding/performance appraisal/evaluation time. There are hundreds of jobs/projects/assignments in the world of work. But the employee has chosen this one for something other than the pay cheque. Ask them point-blank, "Why are you passionate about this work?" or "For what reason other than the pay cheque do you do this job?"

2. PERFORMANCE

There is no better than adversity. Every defeat, every heartbreak, every loss, contains its own seed, its own lesson on how to improve your performance the next time.

Malcolm X

The true measure of the value of any business leader and manager is performance.

Brian Tracy

An ounce of performance is with pounds of promises.

Mae West

The biggest hurdle that team building and engagement have faced has been connecting them to KPIs (Key Performance Indicators), as we well know that profit management is a key driver in any business. Looking for funds and time to spend with your team often requires a clear line to profit and performance. Here are a couple of activities that can help to "make the case," as well as allow you as the manager to know how your team is progressing using metrics.

PROFIT PER X

Intelligences: Intrapersonal, Logical/Mathematical, Naturalist

Time: 30 min to 1 hr

You need: Pen/pencil, paper, calculator (if you're like me)

No matter what business you are in, you need to be able to define and measure your performance with this KPI. Calculate and measure your "profit per x." It could be profit per units sold, number delivered, people served, etc. The basic formulas for expressing profit are:

- Gross Sales - Cost of Goods Sold = Gross Profit

- Gross Profit/Sales = Gross Profit Margin

- (Selling Price - Cost to Produce)/Cost to Produce = Mark up Percentage

Compare the results year over year to see how the engagement (among other things) of your employees is affecting profit.

TEST TRACK

Intelligences: Logical/Mathematical, Visual/Spatial, Naturalist

Time: 30 min to 1 hr

You need: Pen/pencil, paper, display board/Bristol board

Managing performance is often about managing deadlines. Create a master sheet with realistic project deadlines. Set a goal for you/your team that defines percentage of times expectations are met or exceeded in terms of meeting deadlines. Review your progress regularly. For more supervisory leadership tasks with your team, try this. Meet at the beginning of the day. Assign tasks and deadlines to achieve them on a master sheet. Have staff sign back in upon completion of the tasks. Do this once a week for the same tasks and challenge the team to improve their performance times. Talk about what they did to improve their efficiency and effectiveness without compromising quality. Provide a prize for the entire team if they can improve performance numbers by x percent.

GOAL SETTING

Intelligences: Intrapersonal, Bodily/Kinesthetic, Verbal/Linguistic, Logical/Mathematical

Time: 20 min

You need: Pen/pencil, paper

Take a meeting every quarter and set some goals with your team. Make sure that they follow good goal writing format (SMART: Simple, Measurable, Achievable, Realistic, and Time Dependent). Track and report to the team on a regular basis how you are performing toward those goals. One way to do this is to have team members set personal mini-goals that help them to move things forward on the team's behalf; check in on those regularly within the quarter.

IT'S BEEN SAID…

Intelligences: Interpersonal, Bodily/Kinesthetic, Verbal/Linguistic

Time: 20 min

You need: Nothing specific is required for this activity

Everyone likes to hear when they are performing well. Unfortunately, in today's busy workplace it's not always data that is shared. Connect with a partner department and solicit from their manager specific examples of employees who have been seen performing well (you can reciprocate by sharing the same about that manager's people). Then, share these examples with your team at a meeting. Ensure that the examples are authentic and measured, and that a single person is not always being appreciated. Ensure that you "share the love."

3. EFFORT

Strength and growth come only through continuous effort and struggle.

Napoleon Hill

Individual commitment to a group effort—that is what makes a team work, a company work, a society work, a civilization work.

Vince Lombardi

Satisfaction lies in the effort, not in the attainment, full effort is full victory.

Mahatma Gandhi

Building an engaged team is as much about what we do with the members, as what we stop them from having to do. Often we start things because they matter at that point, but through time and new protocols in our business things change. These changes often see us with "leftovers" of activity that cause unrequired efforts. These extra efforts often cause discontent. So as a leader of your team, it is important to occasionally assess not only what they should be doing more of but also what they can be doing less of.

STOP IT

Intelligences: Intrapersonal, Logical/Mathematical, Naturalist

Time: 30 min to 1 hr

You need: Pen/pencil, paper

Being an effective team is not always about what you are doing, but often what you can stop doing. Take a moment with your team to explore things that they can stop doing. Brainstorm and build action plans around what they can do less of. Think of the things you want to remove around the pillars of: not congruent with our purpose; more efficient ways to accomplish; wastes time that could be allocated elsewhere. Be brutal in your analysis and be open to what is said; look for the nuggets of wisdom about what can be stopped. This exercise is not meant to talk about individual behaviours, but rather workflow.

WASTEOID

Intelligences: Logical/Mathematical, Naturalist, Verbal/Linguistic

Time: 30 min once a day/3 days and 1 hr

You need: Pen/pencil, paper

There are only so many minutes in a workday. Being the most efficient with those minutes can be a tipping point for success. Take three days and have your team track the tasks they do in the run of a day. Then, sit together and look through a critical lens and discover what is a waste of time. Use the measurement of looking at: what are we duplicating; can I outsource this; not the best use of my skills; etc. Remove or reallocate what is a waste of team energy.

HOW DO WE DO IT...

Intelligences: Interpersonal, Naturalist, Visual/Spatial

Time: 30 min to 2 hr

You need: Whiteboard, markers

Doing less of stuff we don't want to do is critical, but also figuring out how to engage our efforts in doing more of the stuff we want to accomplish as a team is equally critical. This is a simple consulting tool that helps you fan out those ideas. It's easy to use and enables you as the manager to establish specific actionable items your team can do. What's even better is that team members had a hand in helping to co-create the future efforts of the entire team.

The event takes about 30 minutes to a couple of hours, depending on the depth you wish to take the assessment. Gather your team around a table. Pick one of your team goals and write it on the left-hand side of the whiteboard. Then, you are going to work your way across the whiteboard by expanding on the goal with the question, "How do we do that?" For example, your goal is to sell 1,000 more widgets this fiscal. That's written on the left-hand side of the board. From that, draw an arrow for each answer to the question, for instance, arrow 1) Make twenty more cold calls a day; 2) Update the website, 3) Connect with three existing customers a day and inquire about reordering, etc. Then, from each of those arrows, ask the same question and continue to break it down further. For example, 2) Update the website would include arrows that say 2.1) Include an online order button for widgets, 2.2) Enhance social media marketing strategy, 2.3) Invest in Search Engine Optimization, etc. Continue to ask the same question for each arrow until you have exhausted the possibilities. Then, compile a list of sequential actions to reach your goal.

MANAGE THE CHATTER

Intelligences: Interpersonal, Bodily/Kinesthetic, Logical/Mathematical

Time: 5 min to 20 min

You need: Nothing specific required for this activity

An open-door policy is great; however, if you don't adequately manage the employees who take advantage of it, you might be left with no time to do your work. When someone comes to your office to meet, try this. Get up from your desk and move to greet them at your door. Try to make it a quick standing conversation, or sit with them in the "guest" chairs of your office. If the conversation is finished and you are heading into unproductive chatter, pick up your coffee mug and ask them if they want to walk with you to get a coffee. Then, say goodbye in the public place while you grab your cup of java.

90/10 RULE

Intelligences: Interpersonal, Bodily/Kinesthetic, Naturalist

Time: 5 min

You need: Nothing specific is required for this activity

It's easy to get stuck in the downward spiral of complaints. Set a new policy that at team meetings your conversations become solutions-focused. Spend 10 percent of your time defining the problem, and 90 percent of the time discussing solutions. Take a few minutes to write down some questions that you can pose to help refocus your team toward discovering solutions. For example, "Yes, and where do we start with fixing the gap?" Or,

"OK, so we agree the problem is rooted in x. What in your experience has helped solve that before?" Your ability to move the conversation to solutions will eventually define the problem 100 percent, but you will be actively solving it while you get there.

4. BEST PRACTICE

We are what we repeatedly do. Excellence, then, is not an act, but a habit.

Will Durant

Best practices are those practices that generally produce the best results or minimize risk.

Chad White

Innovation and best practices can be sown throughout an organization—but only when they fall on fertile ground.

Marcus Buckingham

Often in business we already have the solutions that work. I heard one business leader say at a private business event, "Let's just sell what we have on the truck." You see, they were making custom IT solutions, and the margin on those were not as good as the IT solutions that lined the shelves of their "trucks." We can learn from that when it comes to team engagement. Often we have lots of solutions that have worked, and they have found their way to the dark corners. Every now and again, take some time to explore what has worked to find solutions for what's on the table now. Try these activities that speak to the adage of "not reinventing the wheel."

DO IT AGAIN

Intelligences: Interpersonal, Bodily/Kinesthetic, Visual/Spatial

Time: 20 min

You need: Pen/pencil, sticky notes

Host a meeting with your team and ask them think of the three best things they used to do but don't seem to be still doing anymore. Have each member write those things on a sticky note. As they place the sticky note up for all to see, have them explain why these things were good, and how they helped. After everyone has had a chance to present their "things," instruct each team member to put three check marks on the sticky notes around the table to vote for the things to resurrect. Often, when we get busy good things fall to the wayside.

WE ROCK

Intelligences: Logical/Mathematical, Naturalist, Visual/Spatial

Time: 30 min to 1 hr

You need: Pen/pencil, paper/Bristol board

Divide a sheet of paper in half lengthwise into two columns. In the right column header put "We Rock At." Then, have your team list things that they are amazing at doing under that header (e.g., we communicate well, we support people who need help, we meet deadlines, we have great skills in X, etc.). Then, for the left-hand column header put "Stuff to Break." In this column list pervasive problems the team is encountering. Have the team identify the things they rock at that will enable them to break the stuff that is a problem. Then build quick action plans to use what your team rocks at to demolish that which is causing issues.

BENCHMARK ANALYSIS

Intelligences: Interpersonal, Naturalist, Logical/Mathematical, Intrapersonal

Time: 30 min to 2 hr

You need: Pen/pencil, paper

Knowing how well others are doing and then comparing (honestly) how we are doing by identifying gaps and advantages helps to focus our team efforts toward meaningful work actions.

In this analysis, bring your team together and select an internal (i.e., another like department) or external (i.e., competing company) benchmark that is comparable to the work your team is doing. Bring your team together and decide what metrics you wish to use to compare your team to the benchmark. Then study through comparable and relevant data: interviews, online searches, surveys, financial reports, occupational health data, etc., that will uncover performance gaps between the two. From there, explore the benchmark's processes and uncover the differences between your practice and theirs. Next, make suggestions for performance changes that can close the gap. Create an implementation strategy and monitor your team's performance. Set goal posts for performance change with measurable outcomes. Review and retool the strategy.

MENTOR MAGIC

Intelligences: Interpersonal, Bodily/Kinesthetic, Musical

Time: 20 min to 1 hr

You need: Nothing specific is required for this activity

Do you have someone on your team who is particularly awesome at a task? Let them know it. Explain to them why what they do demonstrates excellence, and why how they do it makes them a benchmark for the rest of the team. Then, invite them to provide a bit of an in-service on their awesome skill for the rest of the team. You will move the needle by people identifying improvements they can make in their practice, transferring knowledge, and celebrating each other's abilities.

FIVE-YEAR-OLD INTERVIEW

Intelligences: Intrapersonal, Verbal/Linguistic, Logical/Mathematical, Visual/Spatial

Time: 30 min to 2 hr

You need: Whiteboard, markers

If you have ever hung out with a five-year-old, you'll know that they are masters of the "why" questioning strategy. For every answer that you give them, they turn it into a question as to "why?" For example, "Okay, get your boots on we are going to the store." "Why are we going to the store?" "To get some bread and cheese." "Why do we need bread and cheese?" "Because I'm making grilled cheese for lunch." "Why are we making grilled cheese for lunch?" You get the idea!

In business we use a similar strategy with our teams to uncover root causes of problems as well as bench strengths. To do this, write the thing you want to evaluate on the left-hand side of the whiteboard. Then ask yourself why for that item. Write down two responses. Then ask yourself why for each of those responses, and write down two responses to those. Continue in this manner so that you are five whys deep into the questioning. When you reach the end of the why fan, you will have uncovered root causes of either why you are successful (so you can duplicate or reapply those strategies) or where your problems are (and you can develop strategies to remedy those).

5. CONNECTIONS

If you want to go fast, go alone. If you want to go far, go together.

African Proverb

The most important things in life are your connections to other people.

Tom Ford

The business of business is relationships; the business of life is human connection.

Robin Sharma

A key driver for teams to find their way together is building in the opportunity for them to find and create connections with one another. An effective team need not only be aligned on the vision and the work of the team but also on who the members are within the team.

Spend some time creating those connections both professionally and personally. Here are a couple activities that will help your team to create those points of connections.

COMMONALITIES

Intelligences: Interpersonal, Bodily/Kinesthetic, Naturalist, Musical, Logical/Mathematical

Time: 20 min

You need: Pen/pencil, paper, prizes

A quick activity that can be fun to play with your team is the game of Commonalities. Once people are aware of common connections, it becomes harder for them to be a negative force against someone in the team. The game works like this: at a meeting, take your first 5 minutes to play this. Break your team in to groups of 3 to 10 (you should have at least 3 mini teams). Task the teams in the allotted time of 2 minutes to come up with as many commonalities as they can among the people in their mini team. They have to be things that you can't tell by looking at them (e.g., we all have hair or eyes are a no go). Commonalities have to be things like, we've all travelled outside of the country, we all have kids who play hockey, we all are vegetarian, etc. Give prizes for the largest lists, most obscure/strange/unique commonality, or funniest commonality.

COFFEE TALK

Intelligences: Interpersonal, Intrapersonal, Verbal/Linguistic

Time: 20 min

You need: Coffee Talk Questions (book), coffee

This is a great activity that can be done one-on-one or as a large team. Create your own open-ended statements/questions (or download the book). Invite one member of your team to have coffee with you, or gather the whole team and break them up into pairs. Share a statement such as, "My favourite thing to do on my spare time is…" or, "My dream vacation is…" Give each person 60 seconds or so to answer the question then switch roles. Take turns going first. Do five to seven questions/statements. This activity is great because it's quick and easy to do, all the while delivering to the attentive leader lots of information about the team members.

WHERE'S WALDO

Intelligences: Naturalist, Visual/Spatial, Interpersonal

Time: 20 min to 1 hr

You need: Map of the world, push pins, two different coloured stacks of cards/sticky notes

Maybe it's because I'm Canadian and winters are cold, but one thing I noticed is that people love to travel. Everyone travels for different reasons: beaches, adventure, history, family, or attractions, to name a few. In this simple activity, you post a map of the world. Have two different coloured cards (or sticky notes). Instruct your team to place on the "red" card places they have visited. On the card, also write their name and their favourite thing they saw/did there. Then, on the "yellow" card post it to places they'd like to go. On this card they should write their name and the reason they'd like to travel there. This is a great activity to share dreams and visions as well as to create connections. You can also use this activity to start a conversation about how we bring visions into reality (i.e., how they envisioned going somewhere and what action steps they took to get there.)

PPT OF ME

Intelligences: Interpersonal, Naturalist, Verbal/Linguistic

Time: 20 min

You need: Computer, projector, screen

This is a particularly good one for co-located and virtual teams (as well as traditional teams). Create a list of ten things that speak to your team's common features inside and outside the workday. Share the list of ten things with each person and assign a new person for the beginning of a meeting to share their list (or you could have everyone share the same day if you like). Each person will make a ten slide deck, with one slide dedicated to answering one of the ten questions. Each slide will include photos and maybe some text to explain their answer. They will then present the slides to the team. Some questions that you might use that will create commonalities include: What is your favourite place to go out to eat? Where did you grow up, and why was it great? What is your favourite thing to do outside of work for fun?

6. GOALS

Setting goals is the first step in turning the invisible into the visible.

Tony Robbins

When it is obvious that the goals cannot be reached, don't adjust the goals, adjust the action steps.

Confucius

Stop setting goals. Goals are pure fantasy unless you have a specific plan to achieve them.

Stephen Covey

Creating engagement is about your team members knowing they are involved in something and having clear, measurable points they can aim for to know that they are helping to move toward that point. Durations for goals can and should be short (daily/weekly), medium (monthly/quarterly), and long term (annually/five-year). Create regular conversation that is goal-oriented with your team from morning/toolbox talk meetings to planning retreats. Ensure you are guiding the team to where they are going with specific actions they make to get there.

A good model for writing or explaining goals is to ensure that they are SMART (*Simple* everyone can understand them; *Measurable,* it can be quantified so you know you got there; *Achievable Attainable,* it is possible to do it; *Realistic,* we have the skills/tools to get it done; and [PS *Time Dependant* we have a set date/time for completion).

ROLL OUT THE MARKERS

Intelligences: Naturalist, Bodily/Kinesthetic, Visual/Spatial, Logical/Mathematical, Musical

Time: 20 min

You need: Coloured markers, long roll of paper

One of the best ways to figure out how to achieve your end goal is to reverse engineer it. Once you have a clear and measurable goal, take the time to go backward from it to figure out the steps to get there. Here is what you do: Get a roll of paper about the length of your boardroom table and a pack of markers. Draw a long black timeline along the length in the middle of the paper. At one end of the black line, write "now" and the other end write your "goal." Now with your team, visualize the future as though you have already achieved the "goal." On the timeline, write the steps in the order you took to get there. Once the team has exhausted the major steps that were taken to reach the goal, take some time to dig down into the actions toward those big steps. When you are finished collect the data into an action strategy and share, manage, and design your team's tasks to getting there.

AXES, DARTS, AND RANGES

Intelligences: Interpersonal, Bodily/Kinesthetic, Visual/Spatial

Time: 1 hr to 3 hr

You need: Varies by activity chosen

No matter what way you approach it, goal setting is hitting targets. Setting a goal needs to be measurable to make it a goal, that's why the "measurable and timely" parts are so key to goal setting.

If you are looking for a fun way to spark a conversation about goal setting, grab a dart board, head to an axe-throwing bar, a pool hall, or a shooting range with your team. Any of these locations will give you a great metaphor for goal setting. Take a few minutes when you get there to do some ideating around your goals. Post your goals at the centre of the targets (i.e., the pockets of the pool table, the centre of the dart board, etc.). Then have the team work on hitting those targets. Spend some time talking about what skills, traits, and behaviours it takes to hit those goals. Create a master list of behaviours it takes to hit your team's goals. Coach and manage your team on a regular basis with that list.

WORST-CASE SCENARIO

Intelligences: Interpersonal, Bodily/Kinesthetic, Verbal/Linguistic, Logical/Mathematical

Time: 20 min to 1 hr

You need: No specific materials required for this activity

Fear is the major barrier to achieving your goals. Humans seem to very easily run down the rabbit hole of why things won't work. Instead of combatting the goal, try to establish clarity as to why you are fearful of the "catastrophic" outcome. By spending some time talking about our worst fears about the goal, we can begin to gain clarity toward the goal and build proactive and contingency responses to those fearful outcomes.

Sit with your group. Set an intentional question about your goal such as, "What is the worst thing that could happen if we didn't achieve "goal"?" Have the group brainstorm about the worst-case scenarios. Do this by going around the table so that everyone can voice their examples (and remember this is a brainstorm session). Take note of common themes and particular statements by team members that express their fears of goal failure. Then jot those down on a whiteboard and come up with solutions for those fears. Spend 10 percent of your time talking about the problems and 90 percent talking about the solutions.

TOOLBOX TALK

Intelligences: Interpersonal, Bodily/Kinesthetic, Visual/Spatial, Naturalist

Time: 30 min to 1 hr

You need: Tools (photographs or real)

You've heard your mom say, "Don't reinvent the wheel," right? Goal achievement is not different. You already have most, if not all, the tools in your toolbox already. It's a matter of discovering, naming, and reapplying them.

Get your group together and spend some time talking about a goal they have personally achieved. Have them then identify three skills, traits, or behaviours that enabled them to win that goal. Then, as a team identify a couple of goals that they have won. Do the same practice of identifying the skills, traits, and behaviours that worked best for the team to accomplish that goal. Now, pull out your new goal. Inquire of all the skills, traits, and behaviours that were identified (aka our tools in our toolbox, you can use the photos or real tools to illustrate), what ones can be applied to this goal? Use those applications to help coach and manage the workflow toward attainment of your goal.

DUNKER ROONEY

Intelligences: Bodily/Kinesthetic, Logical/Mathematical, Visual/Spatial

Time: 30 min to 1 hr

You need: Dunk tank, baseballs, a willing manager

Goal setting is a continuous reminder of progress and actions needed to achieve success. Creating a visual hook to the goals helps team members to revisit them. Creating a compelling and unique hook will add energy to their cognitive recall.

Throughout the week, deliver a baseball to each of your team members and tell them that they are really important. Rent a dunk tank and have it delivered and covered in your company parking lot. Put a poster/sign on the target of one your team goals for the quarter. Send a group email or text and have the group meet you in the parking lot with their baseballs. Then, with you sitting on the dunk seat, tell your team that you want them to hit the stated goal (aka target) so badly that you dare them to do it. When everyone has thrown their allotted balls, talk about what it will take for the team to hit their goal.

7. FAMILY

Aim high, work hard, and love your family.

Deborah Roberts

Never forget, your family should always have priority over your work.

Mary Kay Ash

Love your family, work super hard, live your passion.

Gary Vaynerchuk

Let's face it, most people don't live for their jobs, they live for their "family." And each person defines that family differently. Whether family is biological or chosen, the common through line is that they are a priority. Be a manager who takes time to celebrate those your employees deem "family." This can be done through family/work events or by creating opportunities for them to attend the events and activities that are important for their family.

The more that "family" understands the work that the employee does and moreover that they are important to that workplace, the more they will support you and your team members. Develop opportunities that speak to the employees collectively. Develop events, opportunities, and installations that support their family.

FAMILY FUN DAY

Intelligences: All, depending on solution chosen

Time: 20 min to 4 hr

You need: Depends on the solution chosen

Take some time to create a simple and fun event that gets the families together. Wrap these around logical seasons, traditions, or holidays. You can do it yourself or gather an ad hoc team to help you to organize an event.

Here are some great events that you can organize: Tailgate Party, Egg Hunt, Holiday Gift Giving, Pot Luck, Olympic Games, Scavenger Hunt, Movie Theatre Rental, Day at the Zoo, Photo Day with your Pet, Community Service Day, Beach Party, Escape Room, Back to School Party, Haunted House, Holiday Bake-a-thon, and Community Garden.

RETRO BOWL

Intelligences: Interpersonal, Bodily/Kinesthetic, Visual/Spatial, Naturalist, Musical

Time: 20 min to 4 hr

You need: Bowling alley, tacky bowling shirts, silk screen company

A fun way to engage a whole "family" is to have a #TBT event. Sit with your ad hoc team and plan an event that throws back to a time in history, not like pioneers' history, maybe the 70s or 90s. Organize an event that was all the rage. Here is an idea for a retro bowling night. (Other retro events could include: Disco, Roller Skating, Gaming Night, Sock Hop, Barn Dance, or Bonfire/Hayride.)

For the Retro Bowl get some really tacky bowling shirts made with your company logo and people's names. Rent out the local bowling alley and hike down together for a retro bowling tournament. Serve hotdogs and beer (real or root), crank a little Twisted Sister, and turn on the black lights to give this party a little retro "charm."

IT'S A BIG LIFE

Intelligences: Interpersonal, Naturalist, Bodily/Kinesthetic, Intrapersonal

Time: 10 min to 8 hr

You need: Nothing specific required for this activity

Find a way to connect with your employees about things they are passionate about beyond their job. Find ways to help them to champion those things (e.g., conducting a fundraiser for their charity of choice, covering their shift while they watch their child's sport match). If something huge is happening around a personal passion, it's hard to focus at work. If something at work can help bolster a personal passion, it will engage the employee because they feel more connected to work.

CARDBOARD ARCADE

Intelligences: Interpersonal, Naturalist, Bodily/Kinesthetic, Logical/Mathematical, Visual/Spatial

Time: 2 hr to 4 hr

You need: Medium-size cardboard boxes, markers, craft paper, balls/toys/etc., glue/tape/etc., scissors, projector/screen/device (i.e. Phone)

Connecting with those you care about shouldn't be a game of chance, but playing games of chance with those you care about is a great way to connect. This activity is inspired by a young boy named Caine from California. In true entrepreneurial spirit, he decided to take a bunch of cardboard boxes and mash 'em up together with some other cool toys to build Caine's Arcade (google it; you can watch the documentary they made about his story).

In this event, families build an arcade game. You can do this one of two ways. First is to provide a moving-sized box to each employee with a link to the *Caine's Arcade* documentary to share with their family and an invitation to a "date" when all families will join together with their arcade game and play together with a catered lunch. They are to build their game together at home and bring it to the event. Second, you can invite families (or break up into teams within your workplace), show them the trailer of the movie, provide the supplies they need, and give them a time frame to build their arcade on-site. Then of course, let the games begin!

8. CREATIVITY

If you want creative workers, give them enough time to play.

John Cleese

Creativity is intelligence having fun.

Commonly attributed to Albert Einstein

You combine hard work, creativity, and self-determination, and things start to happen.

Sophia Amoruso

Teams need to develop their creative muscles. The way you are currently doing business is not the most efficient and effective; moreover, there are new ideas and opportunities for products and services to better meet your customers' needs. Information is increasing at exponential rates, the time it takes to get products and services to market is faster than ever, and our ability to share electronically/online has never been easier.

Leaders and managers who embrace creativity and encourage it among their team members have the ability to become the forerunners in this innovation. So taking time to work with your team in developing their creative muscles will help to fill your toolkit with ideas and opportunities to flesh out possible innovations.

MONET'S CANVAS

Intelligences: Interpersonal, Bodily/Kinesthetic, Visual/Spatial, Intrapersonal, Musical

Time: 1 hr to 3 hr

You need: Paint, canvas, water, brushes, jars or cups to hold water, clean rags for drying brushes

Paint nights have been an explosive success. They are used as fundraisers (and a great place to grab a glass of wine with friends). Taking the concept of the paint night and bringing it to your office can help you to discover new and exciting things about your team, its products/services and even vision.

Bring in some small canvases, acrylic paints, brushes, and jars/cups of water for rinsing brushes, and clean rags for drying brushes. Get each member of your team to paint a picture based on your "key prompt." Some key prompts you could use include: Paint a picture of the strength you bring to the team, or paint a picture of where we will be as an organization in 5 years. Once all the paintings are complete, set up a "gallery opening," share beverages in stemware, and have each artist explain their masterpiece. Have a conversation about each piece and uncover the importance/value its message can bring to answering your "key prompt." Finally, combine those paintings together to form a patchwork quilt of your team's vision and hang it in your office.

LANYARD BEDAZZLING

Intelligences: Interpersonal, Bodily/Kinesthetic, Visual/Spatial, Intrapersonal, Musical

Time: 30 min to 1 hr

You need: Bedazzler, gems, lanyards

Looking to create team identity and connection through a visual and physical action, then bedazzle.

Set your team apart from the others in your cubicle nation by bedazzling your lanyards with plastic jewels and other bling. Make this the treasure at the end of a measurable business outcome and lock the Bedazzler in a "treasure chest" for all to see. When you hit the goal, crack open the chest and dazzle each other! While your team is bedazzling, ask questions about the things that they did to reach that goal, how did they have to get creative to move toward that goal, etc. Help your team to realize and discuss how they worked together as the key to their success.

1. COMPETITION

Competition is a by-product of productive work, not its goal. A creative man is motivated by the desire to achieve, not by the desire to beat others.

Ayn Rand

The healthiest competition occurs when average people win by putting above average effort.

Colin Powell

Talent wins games, but teamwork and intelligence win championships.

Michael Jordan

Competition is a natural thing. We have forever, as a species, competed for space, food, water, and more. There are times as a team that we need to learn how to effectively compete with each other as well as our natural industry opponents. To be a player, you have to know how to compete. This involves learning to win, lose, encourage, trust, strategize, and more.

Consider your team for a moment. How do they compete in their workplace? When do they compete outside the workplace? What is the response of those who win and lose? Where can your team benefit from learning positive competitive skills? Below you will find some activities you can do as a team that enhance (among other things) the ability to compete.

TEAM BENCH STRENGTH

Intelligences: Intrapersonal, Logical/Mathematical, Verbal/Linguistic, Naturalist, Visual/Spatial

Time: 20 min to 1 hr

You need: spreadsheet

Assessing our human resources is a great place to start when we are establishing a strategic approach to winning in our business. Creating competitive advantage means that you have the right people doing the right things at the right time. As a manager you need to assess your team members' skill strengths so you know where to best allocate their efforts on behalf of the team.

A quick exercise you can do to accomplish this is to build a spreadsheet with your team members' names down the first column. Across the top of the spread sheet, list the skills required to accomplish the project at hand (i.e., C++, JavaScript, Customer Service). Then for each person do an assessment of their abilities based on that skill criteria. Give them a check mark if they have the skills and leave it blank if they don't yet have a skill. This assessment will let you know who to best place into pieces of the project, as well as gaps that you may need to fill to accomplish the task.

CONSOLE OLYMPICS

Intelligences: Intrapersonal, Bodily/Kinesthetic, Visual/Spatial, Logical/Mathematical, Musical

Time: 20 min 3 hr

You need: Bristol board, game console/device

Finding ways to engage teams that are in the same office and collocated can be a challenge. A great way to share an experience when your schedules don't match up to get together for a challenge is to use existing game challenges. Could be a card game like solitaire (give points for every card they get onto the ace) or video games.

Console: You can easily set up a gaming challenge using inexpensive or online gaming solutions. If you check your local online seller (i.e. kijiji, e-bay, etc.), pawn shop, or even your basement, you'll find lots of old gaming consoles). Bring them into the lunch room and set up an Olympic-styled challenge, or even just a grid, and track people's best scores. Choose an assortment of games. Have a weekly challenge and provide prizes and bragging rights.

Online: Go online and find a site that has really easy to play games or an app that works on Apple and Android. Then, invite your team to have an Olympic Game challenge by breaking into countries (sub-teams) and tracking scores. Give out medals if you like, or just dish out bragging rights. This is a great adaptation for virtual teams; just pick your favourite social networking site to post scores.

LIVING INFLUENCE

Intelligences: Intrapersonal, Verbal/Linguistic, Visual/Spatial, Logical/Mathematical, Naturalist

Time: 20 min to2 hr

You need: Whiteboard, markers

How we influence others helps push our competitive position forward. Competing against other departments or companies often has to do with how well we can influence potential customers, stakeholders, suppliers, etc. Taking some time with your team to find out where your efforts are best utilized for influencing others toward your specific team goals is time well invested for many teams. Here is a quick exercise you can use to assess your team's influence and where you should be investing your energies.

On a whiteboard, draw three concentric circles as though you have dropped a pebble in still water and have three distinct radiating circles. In the centre circle write, "Things we can influence and control"; in the second circle write, "Things we can influence but have no control over"; and in the third and final circle write, "Things we have no influence and control over." Now brainstorm a list of issues you are currently facing on a separate whiteboard. Once you have exhausted that brainstorm list, then add each of the issues to their appropriate circle on the first whiteboard. This will give you a better understanding of how to utilize your time and efforts as a team toward influencing change as part of your competitive strategy.

BUSINESS IS A GONG SHOW

Intelligences: Interpersonal, Bodily/Kinesthetic, Musical

Time: 10 min

You need: Gong, noise makers, Bristol board, prize

Creating competition need not be an event. Rather, it can just be a symbolic tool that reminds and shares with the team that they have won.

A great way to do this is to set up a metal gong in the centre of your sales team's space. Every time they make a sale, they get to go up and hit the gong. You can support their success either by everyone else clapping and cheering or hand out kazoos or harmonicas and have everyone else join in a chorus of cacophony. You can build on the challenge: have your individual team members keep track of their sales and have a prize for goal attainment or overall top score.

2. CONVERSATION/NETWORKING

Networking is more about "farming" than it is about "hunting." It's about cultivating relationships.

Dr. Ivan Misner, BNI

The richest people in the world look for and build networks. Everyone else is looks for work.

Robert Kiyosaki

What makes networking work is that it sets up win-win situations in which all parties involved get to take something home. Networking is a sharing process. Until you understand that, you won't have much of a network.

Earl G. Graves Sr.

Developing engagement is a fine art that is benefited by conscious application of good conversation. Building opportunities for thoughtful connection through conversation will help to enhance your team's engagement with one another.

Through conversation team members learn how to work together, trust, and problem-solve (among other skills). This connection creates humanity among the team, which in the long run will help to reduce or minimize interpersonal relationship issues. There are a host of other reasons why conversation should be a cornerstone of your team's engagement strategy (who knows, maybe that will be a book in and of itself). For now, let's get talking and sharing more often.

COFFEE BAR

Intelligences: Interpersonal, Bodily/Kinesthetic, Visual/Spatial, Naturalist

Time: 1 hr to 2 hr

You need: Coffee, blackout drapes/garbage bags, shag carpet/lamps/chairs

Let's turn the coffee break into an opportunity to connect. Host a meeting and build a coffee bar in your office. Here's how: Shut your office door, put garbage bags up on your windows and bring in your table lamps from home (and shag carpet if you have it) to make a groovy atmosphere for a coffee house. Set up a stool in the corner and invite in your team. Pass out some "fancy" coffees and invite each person to take the stool and answer the "groovy question" –(e.g., What are you most excited about for this quarter? or, What was your biggest success so far this year?) Instead of clapping, you can snap your fingers—just like a 70s coffee house.

IDEPTH TOUR

Intelligences: Interpersonal, Bodily/Kinesthetic, Musical, Intrapersonal

Time: 20 min to 30 min

You need: Device with apps

We spend a lot of time online, and even more on our handheld devices. What are we doing when we are there? What has captivated our attention? What does it say about us? Who else is playing that app or planning that renovation? Why not start a conversation and find out.

Have a different member of your team start your meeting by sharing their favourite "out-of-the-way place" in cyberspace or their favourite app. The presenter gets 5 minutes to show why they love this cyberspace place or the functionality/fun of the app. Be sure to continue the conversation after the 5-minute presentation so that you can connect people in your team through shared interests.

POT LUCK

Intelligences: Interpersonal, Bodily/Kinesthetic, Naturalist

Time: 1 hr to 2 hr

You need: Depends on dishes made: knives, forks, plates, glassware, etc.

It works for churches and associations why not your team? The family dinner is an important part of any team. Plus sharing new and exciting things about each other has considerable value to how we see ourselves collectively.

You can have a simple pot luck and have everyone bring in a dish they like, or I like to ramp up the "traditional" pot luck and give some constraints for the dish they bring (i.e., must be from your country of origin, must use only four ingredients, has to contain all food groups) Your creativity is your only constraint.

BRINGING HOME THE KEVIN BACON

Intelligences: Interpersonal, Bodily/Kinesthetic, Logical/Mathematical, Naturalist, Verbal/Linguistic

Time: 1 hr to 4 hr

You need: Nothing specific required for this activity

They say that you can connect any actor or actress in a movie with no more than six degrees of separation from Kevin Bacon. That same premise has been suggested for the rest of the world…you just have to network effectively to find those links. Business success is often about the network of people, trusted advisors, and connections you have. So here is a fun game you can play with your team.

Meeting Version: Create a list of twenty-five names of famous people. Then, break your team into sub-teams of two to three and challenge them to use their network to get to each of those famous people within an allotted time (say 30 minutes). They can call connections, use social networking sites, etc. The sub-team that can accomplish the complete task before the end of the time frame will be declared the winner, or the team that can connect to the greatest number of the names on the list at the end of the time will be the winner. To break a tie, the team with the least total number of degrees of separation will win.

Live Event Version: Attend a networking event or other business event. Hand out a list of three different possible customers to each member of your team. Make it their mission to attend the event and effectively network to gain the contact information/introduction of those three possible customers. Once they have successfully broken the ice for those three, they can see you and gain another list of three. The team member who can connect to the most number of possible customers wins.

EGG HUNT

Intelligences: Interpersonal, Intrapersonal, Bodily/Kinesthetic, Visual/Spatial, Logical/

Mathematical, Naturalist

Time: 20 min to 1 hr

You need: Chocolate eggs

Building fun and spontaneous activities can be a real draw for many members of a team. Here is a great way to have a bit of easy-going fun and spur some great conversation.

Inform your team to meet you at the office for a very important meeting at 8:30 AM, sharp. Set up a chocolate egg hunt around your office, before you leave the night before said meeting. Then, put up crime scene tape on the door so no one enters in the morning. When they all arrive, tell them there has been a reverse robbery and one hundred chocolate eggs were hidden in the office. They need to be found before they melt. Once they have found all the eggs, team members tell one interesting fact about themselves for every egg they found.

3. FUN

Have fun, work hard and money will come. Don't waste time—grab your chances. Have a positive outlook on life. When it's not fun, move on.

Sir Richard Branson

Where people aren't having any fun, they seldom produce good work.

David Ogilvy

People rarely succeed unless they have fun in what they are doing.

Dale Carnegie

Traditionally, we have framed team building as it is about having fun together. There is some wisdom to that, but really it's not the only outcome for a team. It's about all those other concepts you can develop around how human relations work: engagement, agreement, metrics, strategy, communication, trust, etc.

That said, fun is such a central part of any of the activities or initiatives you invest yourself in to develop your team. In addition, fun can be an outcome in itself as well as a contributing tool to develop and engage your team so they can realize other outcomes.

The trick with fun is it is idiosyncratic (i.e., in the eye of the beholder). So when planning a "fun" team building event or activity, do so with the members' sense of "fun" in mind. Just because you think golf is fun doesn't necessarily mean everyone else does. This means that "fun" events usually have to speak to many different intelligences—strategic design of the fun is imperative.

RANDOM LIST OF FUN

Intelligences: All depending on solution chosen

Time: 20 min to 8 hr

You need: Depends on the solution chosen

Here is a list of random things that you can do—just for fun—as a team:

- Rent inflatable sumo suits and battle it out.
- Visit an axe-throwing bar.
- Play laser tag.
- Rent and/or drive go-karts, horse-drawn carriages, luxury cars, a limo.
- Host a cook-off for "best chili."
- Play mini golf or a round of golf.
- Rent a recording studio and record a song.
- Paint pottery (new mugs for the lunch room?).
- Volunteer to walk dogs at the SPCA.
- Have a barbecue in your parking lot.
- Produce a video that celebrates your team.
- Go to an escape room.
- Attend a fancy dress-up dinner together.

- Plant a garden together.
- Play a team sport together.
- Climb at an indoor climbing gym.
- Build a bike and give it to a needy child.
- Have a food truck rally in your parking area and treat everyone to lunch.
- Draw chalk art on the sidewalk.
- Start a book club.
- Have a treasure hunt.
- Lunch and learn with a sommelier (Nudge, nudge. Wink, wink.)
- Learn to juggle.
- Attend a yoga class.
- Get a dunk tank.
- Rent and drive RC cars through a closed course you make.
- Build a sculpture out of cans and then donate them to the local food bank.
- Build a promo video for your team.
- Design a team logo and get shirts/jackets made.

4. PROBLEM-SOLVING

We cannot solve our problems with the same thinking we used when we created them.

Albert Einstein

If you double the number of experiments you do per year you're going to double your inventiveness.

Jeff Bezos

We can complain because rose bushes have thorns, or rejoice because thorns have roses.

Alphonse Karr

When considering key performance behaviours for a team, problem-solving definitely ranks high on the list of must-haves. No matter what business or service you are invested in, you and your team's ability to resolve issues will be an important facet. This is a skill that can be improved through practice and dialogue. Spending time with your team exploring their collective and individual problem-solving skills will likely reap dividends in customer service ratings, safety, and engagement.

There are lots of problem-solving strategies and theories. Acquaint yourself with one and use it as a backdrop in your facilitated dialogue about problem-solving and how "we" do it to improve our workspace and place.

TOUR DE TRIKE

Intelligences: Interpersonal, Bodily/Kinesthetic, Visual/Spatial, Logical/Mathematical, Musical, Naturalist

Time: 40 min to 2 hr

You need: Traffic cone, trikes

One way to set up a great team-building experience that will enable you to talk about problem-solving is to host a continuous improvement style event like Tour de Trike. It enables you to discuss performance improvements as a team using problem-solving to improve a measurable score (time). This discussion within the event becomes great learning material for framing how to solve a problem as a team.

Grab a couple of trikes from the local bike shop and set up either an obstacle course in your parking lot or map out a route around the block for a race (take measures to ensure safe riding), using a traffic cone for the start/finish line. Divide the group up in teams to ride in the Tour de Trike. Once the team has completed the route, add a complication to the challenge. For example, can you shave 30 seconds off your time? From there have the team problem-solve a solution to the issue.

CAUSES THAT AFFECT US

Intelligences: Interpersonal, Visual/Spatial, Logical/Mathematical, Musical, Naturalist, Verbal/Linguistic

Time: 20 min to 2 hr

You need: Whiteboard/paper, markers

Teams need to be able to define their problems and understand the causes and effects that create issues to be resolved. Once your team is able to define the problem, this is a great exercise to discover the causes and effects that can be worked on to remedy/resolve the issue identified.

Collect your team (two to ten people) and book off 1–4 hours, depending on the level of detail you are looking to flesh out with the analysis. Then, on the right-hand side of a sheet of paper (or whiteboard) write down the problem to be addressed. To the left of the problem, draw a fish bone analysis chart (with four to six "ribs"). At the ends of the fish bone ribs, identify the major causes of the problem at hand. Then, analyze the effects of the causes by asking why-related questions and list them down the rib bones. When you have analyzed your causes, look for commonalities throughout the diagram and group them into areas where you can focus your efforts for issue resolution.

WE'RE A BUNCH OF TOOLS

Intelligences: Interpersonal, Bodily/Kinesthetic, Visual/Spatial, Naturalist

Time: 20 min

You need: Tools or pictures of tools

Solving problems is a path to learning. We all have different skills that we apply to solve issues. It's kind of like a big toolbox, and depending on the problem, we pull out the tool we need to get the job done.

Use this metaphor of "tools in our toolbox" to solve problems and put a toolbox on the table in front of your team. Open up the toolbox and show the team the plethora of tools they can choose from. Ask them to choose a tool that represents a skill they are proud of and use when they are solving problems. For example, I choose a hammer because it helps me be precise in driving nails (solutions) where they belong. For a variation, you can present quick, one-paragraph problems and ask what tools (skills) are required to resolve the issue.

ESCAPE ROOM

Intelligences: All, especially Logical/Mathematical, Bodily/Kinesthetic, Interpersonal

Time: 1 hr to 3 hr

You need: Escape room

There are downloadable escape rooms online that you can use with your team, and there is probably a real-life one in your town. Escape rooms are great learning tools for your team to actively engage with the collective practice of solving problems.

Take your team to an escape room and give them the opportunity to work together to escape. As they are working in the room, take note of behaviours, roles, and barriers to their ability to escape and work as a team. Once the event is complete, spend some time talking about how they could have worked differently to escape and what they did really well that moved them forward. You can then apply the escape experience to a problem that needs to be solved at work. Find out what skills and behaviours they can apply from the escape room to help resolve the pervasive problem at work.

5. STRATEGY

Thus, what is of supreme importance in war is to attack the enemy's strategy.

Sun Tzu

Strategy is not really a solo sport—even if you're the CEO.

Max McKeown

I have not failed. I've just found 10,000 ways that won't work.

Thomas Edison

Strategic thinking is often a core skill required by teams. For some senior teams it is a day-to-day tool they utilize, while more front line teams might use it at the beginning of a day to decide on immediate workflow. But no matter which way you cut it, at one point or another the ability to strategize will help teams to have better efficiency and effectiveness in their actions.

These team-building tools that help to encourage strategic thinking can be well applied just before teams head into strategy sessions or as an annual or bi-annual reminder of the importance of strategic thinking toward better workflow outcomes.

BUSINESS OF SPORT

Intelligences: Interpersonal, Bodily/Kinesthetic, Visual/Spatial

Time: 2 hr to 5 hr

You need: Tickets to a sporting event

Coaching a team to success, on and off the field, takes strategy. Some of the best strategic thinkers are professional coaches. Invest in a study session of strategy by taking your team out to a semi-pro or pro sporting event. Before you go, ask your team to take note of moments where the coach or players had to use strategy to accomplish their goals.

After the game, talk to your team about what they saw the sport teams doing right, what it took to win, and how that applies to your upcoming business pursuits. Use the game as a metaphor for business and continue the investment by sending cards with the game ball on it, make jerseys for team events, play a "team" theme song, etc. Make a list of the top strategies you saw at the game, and refer to those as a team as you go forward.

STRATEGIC TRAVEL PLANNER

Intelligences: Interpersonal, Intrapersonal, Visual/Spatial, Naturalist
Time: 20 min to 1 hr
You need: Whiteboard, markers

This tool can be used for planning your career as well as visioning and strategic thinking. Essentially, you are going to map out how to arrive where you want to be over a given time frame. You will list your "destination" on the right-hand side of your whiteboard and list the three to five effort areas that you will have to invest in along the left-hand side. Across the top of the board, break the remaining space into equal parts to represent equal years (i.e., five sections = five years). Now, think through each of the effort areas in sequential order to arrive at the destination. Draw lines from each thought area to the next, lineally as well as where it intersects with other effort areas. When you have finished your analysis, you should have a visual representation of the efforts you will need to take in individual years to arrive at your destination.

SCAVENGER HUNTER

Intelligences: All

Time: 20 min

You need: Paper, pen/pencil, list, stopwatch

Collecting all the items on a list, whether it is a grocery list, gift list, or scavenger hunt list, requires ingenuity and strategy. If you want to help your team members to think strategically, host a scavenger hunt. There are lots of scavenger hunts you can host, from car scavenger hunts to office scavenger hunts.

Here is a simple one you can do in any space. Compile a list of things that your team might be able to find on their person, in their brief case, purse, bag, etc. At your meeting, break your team into equal parts (three to a team is great, or for larger teams maybe the table rounds they are sitting at). Now, have them see how many of each item they can find in 5 minutes. Teams get a point for each item they find (e.g., coin, cellphone, tissue, etc.). Winning team gets a prize or just bragging rights. You can use the scavenger hunt experience to debrief about what strategy the teams used to accomplish the goal. Further the dialogue by finding out what they would change or do the same to create an improved level of success.

INTRANET HUNT

Intelligences: Intrapersonal, Verbal/Linguistic, Logical/Mathematical, Naturalist

Time: 20 min to 2 hr

You need: Intranet, list

For virtual teams or teams that work different shifts (e.g., call centres), try building an intranet scavenger hunt by depositing some clues inside client files or other shared workspaces inside your intranet. Give team members a list of clues as to where to find them. Then set them loose. First person to complete the intranet hunt wins. Or another options is an Internet Hunt. Here set up a challenge for your team to find a list of obscure items online, compile their findings in a PowerPoint or keynote presentation, rip to PDF, and send it to you. The person who finds the most wins. Great fun for virtual teams.

VISION BOARDS

Intelligences: Intrapersonal, Bodily/Kinesthetic, Visual/Spatial, Naturalist, Musical, Interpersonal

Time: 30 min to 1 hr

You need: Paper, pen/pencil/marker, boards/picture frames, stick glue, magazines, scissors

Seeing is believing they say. And there is some research and wisdom to building a visual representation of what you want to accomplish. Take the architects who build scale balsam wood models of the houses they are building, or the artists who do a quick sketch of their paintings before they paint them. Our team success can be like that too if we use the same practices to get to their desired outcomes.

A great activity to build a visual representation/reminder for the team is to build a picture that speaks to a key question. To do this, go to the store and get a bunch of magazines, glue, and scissors. Then, facilitate a discussion around a key question (e.g., What does it take to be successful in our project, or What are the key components of our new building design). Then, have the team members dig through the magazines for pictures that represent the answer(s) to the question. Have each member present their items and have the group agree which items belong on the vision board. Paste those images to the board, talk about why it is a good vision for the question, and then hang it in a place where all can be reminded of the collaborative vision. This can also be a great exercise for performance management if you do individual boards.)

6. COLLABORATION

Competition makes us faster; collaboration makes us better.

Fyrefly

Unity is strength…when there is teamwork and collaboration, wonderful things can be achieved.

Mattie Stepanek

Great things in business are never down by one person. They're done by a team of people.

Steve Jobs

When getting the job done requires more than one person, collaboration is a core competency. Collaboration sees two or more people working together in a harmonious way to complete a task, with each person contributing to its success. While it is about people working together to achieve a goal, collaboration also requires leadership to ensure an egalitarian approach to goal attainment.

Teams have to collaborate within their formal structure as well as with outside vendors. Taking time with your team to hone their collaborative skills will help to ensure smooth running of task completion and goal attainment.

FULL VALUE CONTRACT (FVC) PROJECT CHARTER

Intelligences: All

Time: 30 min to 1 hr

You need: Bristol board, markers

A great start to building collaborative relationships can be pro-actively framed using this simple yet effective behavioural contract. Essentially, the team will suggest, define, and agree to a set of "rules" by which they will work together. This FVC helps your team establish alignment on things like communication, trust, listening, etc. You can pre-frame your team's experience by adding the behavioural construct of your choice, such as collaboration, safety, respect, etc. By doing so, you have a tool that everyone has "signed off on" to manage unwanted and encourage preferred behaviours within your team.

Here's how you do it: place a piece of Bristol board and markers in the centre of the group. Ask them to draw an icon of things that serve as a metaphors for group behaviour that "we" need to do to make our team successful (e.g., ears for listening, weights for working hard, etc.) After each icon is drawn, encourage group members to agree that it is something their group needs to be successful. Once everyone has drawn and explained their drawing, you will have an agreed upon behavioural contract.

AHOY, MATE

Intelligences: Interpersonal, Bodily/Kinesthetic, Intrapersonal, Naturalist

Time: 1 hr to 4 hr

You need: Sail boat, instructor

Outward Bound is one of the premier leaders in leadership development using the outdoors as a training tool. One of their sayings for debriefing an experience is "let the mountains speak for themselves." In other words, sometimes there are experiences so powerful that they confirm the learning, and you don't have to debrief to flesh out the learning. Sailing has that possibility when it comes to collaborative teamwork.

To explore this possibility, set up a day to go sailing. You can learn a lot about collaborative teamwork from the running of a sailing vessel. Encourage the captain to assign tasks and connect those tasks to the smooth running of the sailing day. If you can find smaller vessels, you can break your team up into smaller groups and have them sail their own boat. Check with your local yacht club to see if they have a youth sailing program; if they do, they likely have some Albacore style boats that can do the trick.

COMMUNITY GARDEN

Intelligences: Intrapersonal, Bodily/ Kinesthetic, Visual/Spatial, Naturalist

Time: 20 min to 4 hr

You need: Garden tools, seeds, space, soil (if using planters), etc.

Looking for a team event that takes some time and delivers consistent learning along the way? Setting up a community garden at work might just be the tool you're looking for. The action of taking care of a garden together is a powerful look at collaboration. From planning through to harvest, the actions required to grow a successful garden require all hands on deck.

To set up your community garden, you'll need to acquire some space outside your office (or invest in a hydroponic green wall or tower). Then, together with your team, take some time to plan out what you want to grow. It's really great if you can pass off the project to someone in your team with a green thumb. Following that, take a small budget or borrow the tools and supplies you need. Take a day and plant together, work together to build a schedule to share the watering/weeding, and then harvest and share your bounty. A fun way to do this is to share the produce, and have a pot luck the next day where everyone returns with a dish that includes something from the garden.

7. COMMUNICATION

Communication—the human connection—is the key to personal and career success.

Paul J. Meyer

The single biggest problem in communication is the illusion that it has taken place.

George Bernard Shaw

Communication is a skill that you can learn. It's like riding a bicycle or typing. If you're willing to work at it, you can rapidly improve the quality of every part of your life.

Brian Tracy

This is probably the tipping point for whether your team will be effective or not. Teams that struggle with how to effectively communicate are bound to hit significant snags along the way. Communication is the lifeblood of everything our teams do, from customer service and safety to work requests and reprimands.

Every day there seems to be a new way of communicating; we are inundated with new apps and tools. But they are just that—tools. As a manager, it is in your best interest to develop the core skills around communication. Those core skills can then be transferred into the tool, be it face-to-face or email or text or app. If we can drive home a solid "way" of how to communicate well, we can help usher our team to a place where they will have fewer hiccups because of miscommunication.

TAILGATE LUNCHBOX

Intelligences: Interpersonal, Bodily/Kinesthetic, Logical/Mathematical, Musical

Time: 20 min

You need: Pickup truck, barbecue, lunch fixings, low-organized games, music

They say "a family that eats together stays together." Let's extend that premise to our team. On a regular basis, converge to eat together. It's an informal way to strengthen the communication among team members. Here is a fun way you can connect, get some fresh air, and have some laughs.

Bring in a pickup truck, barbecue, and some root beers on ice. Set up in the parking lot, crank some tunes, set out some lawn chairs, and have a long lunch together. Eat some burgers, hot dogs, and chips, and celebrate your successful outcomes over the quarter. Use this opportunity to celebrate each other and suggest that when the tailgate lunch is over, we are on to our next "game." This way, you can create beginnings and endings to things (a gripe from teams is that their projects don't seem to have logical beginnings and endings. A celebration of the ending and the opening of a new beginning will work toward supporting this concern.)

DJ'S TOP 10

Intelligences: Intrapersonal, Musical, Bodily/Kinesthetic, Interpersonal

Time: 10 min

You need: Electronic device, speaker

It's amazing how music speaks to us. Lyrically songs can inspire us, explain life events, or help us access feelings. Each person has their own playlist that speaks to them. If you looked at the phone of the person next to you, chances are they have a couple playlists on their device. Our team is no different. Teams taking some time for music appreciation can help us to understand and connect with each other.

Have a lunch and share of team members' favourite music. Get one person every Friday to host the DJ's Top 10, where they share the top songs of their lifetime. Play snips of these songs together and send each member of the group an iTunes list of the songs or come up with another "imaginative way" of sharing the music (without infringing on copyright, of course). Have each individual share with the group why specific songs mean something to them, or what message the song conveys to them. Encourage the group to weigh in on the songs' messages and content.

WIKIWORLD & GLOSSARY OF TEAM

Intelligences: Intrapersonal, Verbal/Linguistic, Visual/Spatial, Naturalist

Time: 20 min

You need: Place to post and share

Communicating to new team members can be daunting. There is often vernacular and acronyms that have strong meaning for the team but not for the onlookers or newbies. A fun way to collect the wisdom of the team is to build some tools that explain the unique things the team has to offer. These tools can be used to explain project facets to externals as you have an agreed upon description or definition. These tools can be shared with new members to bring them up to speed—we all know how confusing an acronym-filled meeting can be if you aren't up to speed on the lingo. And finally, these tools can help your team to define what components of the work "mean," creating clarity for problem-solving and communicating needs to one another.

Wikiworld: Looking for a great fast forward event that can be done with a virtual team? Try wikiworld. Essentially, you frame out "something" that needs to be explained about a project, business line, etc., and build a wiki (think *Wikipedia*) about the topic. You can also set up wikis to facilitate different team members getting better acquainted, if ahead of time each person builds their own wiki.

Glossary of Team: We seem to use a lot of vernacular in our business world. Why not use that "unique" quality about your group to build a glossary of your team? Develop and interact with a unique glossary of words or sayings that hold meaning to your group. Post it on a shared document, social networking site, etc., and have people add new terms as they come into the daily life of the group.

8. COMMUNITY

In every community, there is work to be done. In every nation, there are wounds to heal. In every heart, there is the power to do it.

Marianne Williamson

When you choose to give up your time and resources to participate in community work, that's what makes a leader.

Dolores Huerta

Recognize that every interaction you have is an opportunity to make positive impact on others.

Shep Hyken

We are bigger than the work we do. And as a team, it is a great learning tool to be able to give back to our community. In doing so, we increase the social conversation about our place of work. This increase in community esteem about our place of work is shown to increase employee engagement. It's pretty simple: people like to work somewhere that people have a good impression of.

A way to be proactive in building that community esteem about our workplace is to volunteer in that community (also called corporate social responsibility). Find ways to reach out locally and provide service and help. Then, help to ensure that the story is shared to media, up the corporate hierarchy, and even within the team after an event. These feel-good stories help build team camaraderie as well as do some good in your community.

CHARITY CHASE

Intelligences: All depending on actions completed

Time: 20 min to 8 hr

You need: Will depend, based on the solution chosen

Pick a charity close to home and host an annual volunteer day. The act of volunteering for a local charity will enable your team to see the good work they did. Another option is to choose a charity that is associated with your business (e.g., an insurance company helping out their YMCA client). Give of your time, not just a monetary donation; the act of the team working together to "produce something" or "fix something" delivers value to your team and the charity.

Here's how you do it: pick one of your clients or local charities. Plan a "volunteer day" and have your team work to help improve that client's position or service delivery. Help them by doing things on their "to-do list" like painting rooms, building gardens, or installing shelving. Or volunteer your team's expertise (e.g., build a strategic plan or do some accounting for an NFP).

BIKE/TEDDY BEAR BUILD

Intelligences: Interpersonal, Bodily/Kinesthetic, Visual/Spatial, Naturalist, Logical/Mathematical, Musical

Time: 1 hr to 3 hr

You need: Stuffable teddy bears/ bikes in need of assembly, appropriate tools

Looking for a team challenge that delivers something good at the end of the event? Here is a popular one. You can build a learning challenge around any of the core concepts discussed, from strategy to collaboration and goal setting to communication. Frame a challenge of building a bike or stuffing a teddy bear, forming the teams around that concept. Then, debrief the challenge so that the team can learn about the importance of the concept you have chosen.

Following the debrief and connection of the learning to the team event, bring in a social service agency (e.g., Big Brothers Big Sisters) and donate the items you made to them. Have the representative from the agency explain why what the team did will be meaningful to their clients. After the representative is gone with the things your team made, solidify with your team that often when we are working well together on one aspect of our business, we improve another.

CASH MOB

Intelligences: Interpersonal, Naturalist, Bodily/Kinesthetic

Time: 20 min to 2 hr

You need: Cash

A great way to give back to an area/business is to build a "cash mob." Essentially, your cash mob members are given a sum of money each, say ten dollars. Then, collectively you decide on a store that could use the injection of cash. With that decision, the team descends on that small shop and each person spends their allotted sum in that store. (You can combine this with a training retreat as a way to get lunch/snack/dinner/etc.) This is a great way to demonstrate corporate social responsibility as well as make a direct economic impact on a local community.

9. LEARNING

Develop a passion for learning. If you do you will never cease to grow.

Anthony J. D'Angelo

Everyone you will ever meet knows something that you don't.

Bill Nye, the Science Guy

It is utterly false and cruelly arbitrary to put all the play and learning into childhood, all the work into middle age, and all the regrets into old age.

Margaret Mead

If you fail to learn, you fail to grow. Building a team that is driven to learn is a core behaviour that can pay dividends. A manager who role models personal and professional development is a great inspiration to their employees to do the same. Setting up opportunities for employees to learn is a core task of a manager. This can be applied to a staff's performance appraisal, bonus structure, or team events.

Learning is a muscle. People who are constantly learning are exercising their brains to be active. These active brains are an asset to team and business functioning. Allocate a portion of your budget to support people's learning if you can. If you can't do that, look within the team and try to build opportunities to teach each other. This doubles down on the benefits, where your team benefits by learning and also by teaching.

LITERATURE GROUP

Intelligences: Intrapersonal, Verbal/Linguistic, Interpersonal, Naturalist

Time: 20 min to 2 hr

You need: Books

Are there some amazing industry books that you have read or are currently reading that will benefit the work you and your team are doing? Take some time and study the book together. This way you not only get the passive learning of reading the book but also the active learning of discussing the content. Also, you might have a group of people in your team who are working on a specific credential or certification. This might be an opportunity to build a study group with those who are working on the credential and those who have already achieved it.

Here's how you can do it: set up a book group at your work. Read professional writings and have discussion groups around the content of the book. This is a great virtual activity, too, as the eBook can be instantly accessed by everyone and comments can be easily posted on the wall of a social networking site for everyone to engage with.

LEARNING STYLES

Intelligences: All depending on assessment chosen

Time: 20 min to 3 hr

You need: Depends on solution chosen

Taking time to get to know the learning styles of you team can uncover myriad possibilities. You will learn things about how to best communicate, reward/recognize, instruct, and more. Take some time to investigate a personality and learning matrix tool with your team. People love to learn what makes them tick. Here is a list of some tools that might be of interest: 1) Howard Gardner's Multiple Intelligences; 2) Tom Rath's *StrengthsFinder 2.0*; 3) Myers-Briggs Type Indicator; 4) Marcus Buckingham's *StandOut 2.0,*;and 5) DiSC assessment, to name a few.

TEACH US

Intelligences: Interpersonal, Verbal/Linguistic, Bodily/Kinesthetic

Time: 20 min

You need: Paper, pen/pencil

The talents that teams have never cease to amaze. If you take a few moments to interview your members, you will discover that they have amazing "other skills," in addition to the ones they share at work. Here is a way to harness their passions and develop the skills within the rest of your team.

Have each member of your team identify a list of five things that they can teach to the other team members. From each of the lists, build a learning strategy of what you think might be fun, informative, timely, etc., for your team. Build a schedule for "Lunch and Learns" for your team. One member of your team will be the teacher and the rest students. You can incentivize the teacher by giving them a "day off" to prepare their lesson. As well, catering in or a pot luck lunch is another great addition to the learning event.

TOTAL QUALITY MANAGEMENT (TQM)

Intelligences: All depending on course/report selected

Time: 20 min to 8 hr

You need: Depends on solution chosen

This is definitely a management Throwback Thursday. But if you think about it, it really does offer great value. If you are able as a manager to leverage some funds to give each member a small budget to take a course that interests them, it will encourage their engagement at work. They feel connected and appreciated by the firm because they are being supported in discovering their inner interests and talents. To step it up a bit, have your team member report back to the rest of the team what they learned or did with their TQM learning budget.

LUNCH AND LEARN

Intelligences: All depending on course/report selected

Time: 20 min to 8 hr

You need: Depends on the solution chosen

Learning new things is fun. Learning them together can be a great bonding experience and bring lots of laughter. There are plenty of great practitioners in your community who can teach interesting or off-the-wall things, from yoga and meditation to axe throwing and magic tricks.

Do a quick intake of your team to find out fun things that they'd like to learn how to do or know more about. Compile the list and connect with your team to vote on the events they'd most like to try. Build a Lunch and Learn schedule that enables them to learn those things together. Follow up the Lunch and Learns with conversations about what they learned. Have people share photos of where they tried the "thing" in real life, and celebrate those who sign up for more learning about that new skill.

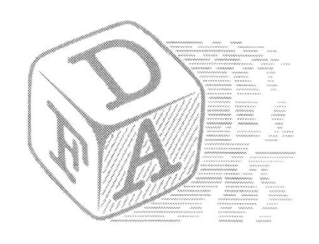

Icebreakers: Breaking the Ice and Energizing Your Team

Here are a bunch of great icebreaker and energizer activities for you to try with you team.

Head over to www.teambuldingactivities.com as lots of the activities included here have companion downloads that you can use right away for only a couple of dollars, and they come with complete directions, a trainer video, and often a team video you can play that is led by the activity's designer. Plus the site is always adding new tools for your team-building practice.

1. PARTICIPANT NAMES

If I could be a _____, I would be a _____ because…

Intelligences: Verbal/Linguistic, Interpersonal, Naturalist

Time: 10 min

You need: No specific equipment required for this activity

Pick a surprising subject to place in the first blank, such as automobile part, vegetable, musical instrument, or something you buy in a grocery store, hardware store, big-box store, etc. Have participants respond with, "If I could be a _____, I would be a _____ because…

PEOPLE POKER (BUY IT HERE)

Intelligences: Bodily/Kinesthetic, Verbal/Linguistic, Interpersonal, Naturalist, Visual/Spatial

Time: 10 min to 15 min

You need: Printed cards (for at least ten people)

In advance, make up some business cards with A, K, Q, J, 10 written in a column on one long edge, with spaces for people to sign their name next to them. Then, at the top of the card include a thing someone could do (e.g., Own a Passport, Play Guitar in a Band, Can Barbecue). Make up a bunch of different cards. Shuffle them and pass five cards out to each person. No person should have two of the same card. Instruct the team to mingle around the room to find people who have done the things listed on their cards. Once they find someone who has done one of the activities on their cards, the first person signs beside the 10, if they find a second, sign at the J, and the third signs at the Q. The players need to use strategy to get the best hand they can in the allotted time. (i.e., five of a kind, full house, etc., where J is jack, Q is queen, K is king, and A is ace.)

MY NAME IS...

Intelligences: Bodily/Kinesthetic, Verbal/Linguistic, Interpersonal, Naturalist, Musical

Time: 10 min

You need: No specific equipment required for this activity

Everyone stands in a circle "Velcro shoulders" style and takes two gargantuan steps back. Ask them to introduce themselves and to think of an activity (verb) they enjoy that also begins with the same letter of their first name. Have them include it in their introduction like this: "Hi, my name is Tyler, and I like to talk." With my verb of choice, I provide a physical action to depict it. Next, the person on my left says her name and verb and performs the action. Then, she says my name and verb and repeats my action. This continues until everyone has had a turn. (Note: I like to do the final whip because it helps me to be sure I have everyone's name down Pat, or was that Cory?)

PEEK-A-WHO

Intelligences: Bodily/Kinesthetic, Logical/Mathematical, Interpersonal, Visual/Spatial, Naturalistic

Time: 10 min

You need: Blanket

Divide the group into two equal parts. Have a co-facilitator or group member grab one corner of a blanket. Hold the blanket up so that it acts as a wall between the two groups. One member from each side comes forward and places their nose against the blanket. On the count of three, drop the blanket. The two people sitting nose to nose must say the name of their counterpart. The first person to say the correct name wins and the other person defects to their side. The activity is over when everyone is on one side or when it's still a lot of fun.

2. BASIC PERSONAL FACTS

TEAM BUILDING 20 (BUY IT HERE)

Intelligences: All intelligences

Time: 10 min to 20 min

You need: Chairs are a nice thing, download the game

Download this game from www.teambuildingactivities.com. It is often free with sign-up for the newsletter. It is a card/dice game that looks like trivial pursuit cards but has questions that will enable your team to get to know each other better. The fun questions are built into categories of Who, What, Where, When, Why, and How. There are also Leadership and Customer Service decks, among others.

AIN'T ME BABY

Intelligences: Verbal/Linguistic, Logical/Mathematical, Interpersonal, Naturalist

Time: 10 min to 15 min

You need: Chairs are a nice thing

Divide into pairs. One partner says as much as he can about himself while the other partner listens for 3 minutes. The listener must remember—without writing or talking—as much as possible about their partner. Then have partners switch roles and repeat for another 3 minutes. Come together as a group and have each set of partners introduce one another, recalling what they just learned.

COFFEE TALK (BUY IT HERE)

Intelligences: Verbal/Linguistic, Logical/Mathematical, Interpersonal, Naturalist, Bodily/Kinesthetic

Time: 10 min to 15 min

You need: Chairs are a nice thing

Divide into pairs. In advance, write a list of open-ended statements or questions on cards. These statements or questions should be framed so that team members can learn something new about the person they are having Coffee Talk with. For example, "My favourite travel destination is…" or, "The best place to eat dinner out is…." Give the team members an allotted time to play (say 5 minutes.) Have one person go first (i.e., answer the first questions). After 30 seconds, call out, "Switch," and the other team member gets to answer the same question. Take turns going first.

COMMONALITIES (BUY IT HERE)

Intelligences: Bodily/Kinesthetic, Logical/ Mathematical, Interpersonal, Verbal/Linguistic, Naturalist

Time: 10 min to 15 min

You need: Pen and paper

Get into groups of four. List on a piece of paper as many commonalities as possible among the group's members. Everything counts *except* what they can tell by looking at each other (e.g., brown hair, wearing jeans, wearing glasses) because that stuff is boring. Share the list with the rest of the group—you can even award prizes.

THUMBS UP (BUY IT HERE)

Intelligences: Verbal/Linguistic, Interpersonal, Naturalist, Bodily/ Kinesthetic

Time: 10 min to 15 min

You need: Chairs are a nice thing

Divide into pairs. Have each partner write a topic on a card. These topics should be framed so that team members can learn something new about the person on the team. For example, "My favourite style of music is…" or, "My favourite TV show is…." Pass the deck of cards to the person on your right. Have them pick up the topic card, read it out loud, then answer it for the group. Others can vote if they, too, like that by putting up one or two thumbs or do not it—no thumbs at all.

WOULD YOU RATHER

Intelligences: Verbal/Linguistic, Logical/Mathematical, Interpersonal, Naturalist, Bodily/Kinesthetic

Time: 10 min to 15 min

You need: Chairs are a nice thing

In advance, write a list of open-ended statements that compare two diverse things. These statements should be framed so that team members can learn something new about the team member. For example, "Would you rather learn to fly a plane or drive a submarine…" or "would you rather sing for AC/DC or ABBA …" Divide into pairs. Pass the deck of cards to the person on your right. Have them pick up the card, read it out loud, then answer it for the group.

"MR. PRESIDENT! MR. PRESIDENT!"

Intelligences: Bodily/Kinesthetic, Logical/Mathematical, Intrapersonal, Verbal/Linguistic,

Naturalist, Interpersonal

Time: 10 min

You need: Pen and paper

With the group sitting in a circle, give each of your learners a few moments to think about summing up who they are in one sentence. For example, mine is, "Tyler Hayden is an amazing keynote speaker and team designer, who is committed to personal development and being a positive influence on the planet and its people." Encourage them to write their sentence down so they can be as concise and effective as possible. Finally, have each member read their summary to the group.

FOUR CORNERS (BUY IT HERE)

Intelligences: Bodily/Kinesthetic, Logical/Mathematical, Interpersonal, Visual/Spatial, Naturalist, Musical

Time: 10 min to 15 min

You need: No specific equipment is required for this activity

Identify four spots for learners to go using soft toys to mark the spots. (If you're inside, corners in a room are convenient (hence, the name of the game). Inform learners that you are going to give them lists of four things in a particular category (for example, potato chips: ketchup, barbecue, regular, or dill pickle), and point toward a different corner with each of the four things. Learners choose which item they would like best (barbecue chips for me!) and go to that corresponding corner. Have learners get to know who in the group values the same things. Make lists of everything and use your imagination. Here are some ideas to get you started: cars, vacation destinations, types of movies, pets, sports on TV, sports to play, outdoor activities, artists, musical bands, and soda pop.

CLAY/DOUGH INTERVIEWS

Intelligences: Bodily/Kinesthetic, Verbal/Linguistic, Interpersonal, Visual/Spatial, Naturalist

Time: 10 min to 20 min

You need: Clay or play dough

Break into new pairs and share with your partner some information about yourself, like where you're from, hobbies, favourite things, etc. Your partner can ask you questions to help prompt you to share specific things. Then your partner makes a representation in clay/dough to show to the group something that you shared with them. Switch up. Then, return as a group and share what you learned.

TWO TRUTHS AND A GOAL

Intelligences: Bodily/Kinesthetic, Logical/Mathematical, Intrapersonal, Verbal/Linguistic, Interpersonal

Time: 10 min to 15 min

You need: Pen and paper (recommended)

Each person tells three stories—two with truthful content about things they have achieved and one that is a goal. Demonstrate how to construct all phrases as goals as if they have already achieved them, much like positive affirmations. For example, "I am a successful businessperson. I am a white-water canoeist. I am a homeowner." The group gets 30 seconds to ask questions about the stories presented. Once the 30 seconds are up, the group votes on which story they feel is the goal.

TWO TRUTHS AND A FIB

Intelligences: Bodily/Kinesthetic, Mathematical, Intrapersonal, Verbal, Interpersonal

Time: 10 min to 15 min

You need: Pen and paper (recommended)

Learners sit in a circle. Provide each learner with the opportunity to make two statements that are true and one that is a fib (a.k.a., a lie). Have learners present individually their truths and lie. If I were to play I might say, "I have gone on a three-day survival expedition buck naked. I have performed CPR and successfully revived a person. I have sold over fifty pieces of artwork in less than a year." Then the group members vote on what they think is the fib. What's my fib? Ask me and I'll tell you. Quick explanations will probably ensue because truth is stranger than fiction.

HAVE YOU EVER?

Intelligences: Bodily/Kinesthetic, Logical/Mathematical, Musical, Verbal/Linguistic, Interpersonal

Time: 10 min to 15 min

You need: No specific equipment required for this activity

Sit the group in a circle and have each person mark their spot with an object, such as a hat, extra sweater, soft toy, etc. Invite one person into the centre and remove their place marker (this way, there will always be one spot short) The person in the centre will ask the group, "Have you ever _____?" The item in the blank will be up to the person in the centre. Anyone sitting in the circle that has done the "_____" will immediately stand up and run to an empty marked spot and sit down. The person remaining without a spot goes to the centre of the circle. The person in the centre will continue to ask, "Have you ever _____?" until they get people to move. Some examples of "have you ever" are: gone on a flight overseas, eaten Thai noodles, had children, bought a car, painted a landscape, jumped out of a plane, gone river rafting, done CPR for real, gone to high school, etc.

TOILET PAPER CONFESSIONS

Intelligences: Bodily/Kinesthetic, Logical/Mathematical, Intrapersonal, Verbal/Linguistic, Interpersonal

Time: 20 min to 30 min

You need: A roll of toilet paper

Sit in a circle and invite everyone to take as much toilet paper as they think they will need from the roll you have supplied. Keep what they're going to do a secret. After everyone has their TP, explain that for every square they have, they are to share a little-known "factoid" about themselves. This activity can take a while, so make sure you've got time.

3. GROUP RE-ENERGIZERS

FULL-BODY PAPER, ROCKS, SCISSORS

Intelligences: Bodily/Kinesthetic, Logical/Mathematical, Visual/Spatial, Naturalist, Verbal/

Linguistic, Interpersonal

Time: 10 min to 15 min

You need: Large, safe space to play

This game is just like the hand version (which you could play, too), except you use your whole body. For paper, you stand with hands above your head and feet together as tall as you can be, like an *I*. For rocks, you crouch down into a ball and hold behind your ankles. For scissors, you are in a jumping jack stance, like an *X*. Split the group into two equal halves. Mark the start and end lines for both groups. Have each group form a football huddle and choose their first and second sign — paper, rocks, or scissors (pick two just in case the first one is a tie). Call the two groups to stand facing each other at their start lines. Group members jump up and down like jumping beans counting, "one, two, three," then shout and strike their pose (paper, rocks, or scissors). The group that wins gives chase to the other group. Anyone tagged before they cross their end line joins the opposing group. Remember: rock beats scissors, scissors beat paper, and paper beats rocks.

CACOPHONY

Intelligences: Bodily/Kinesthetic, Musical, Intrapersonal, Verbal/Linguistic, Interpersonal

Time: 10 min

You need: No specific equipment is required for this activity

Circle up, "Velcro shoulders" style. Ask everyone to think of the coolest noise that they can make with their voice. Then, you go first, following in a clockwise whip, and let everyone perform that sound for 2.36 seconds. Now, holding hands, you start with your noise and continue for 2.36 seconds solo, then squeeze the person's hand on your right. They will make their noise with yours for 2.36 seconds. Continue around the circle until everyone is making their own noise simultaneously for 2.36 seconds. Finally, send a hand squeeze around the circle to create a silent wave. People stop after the person to their right becomes quiet.

BLIND MAN'S CANNONBALL BLUFF

Intelligences: Bodily/Kinesthetic, Logical/Mathematical, Visual/Spatial, Verbal/Linguistic, Interpersonal

Time: 10 min to 15 min

You need: Pen and paper (recommended), one knotted sock (or soft toy) per participant

You will need one knotted sock (or soft toy) per participant. Divide the group into two teams and then partners within each team. Then, give each pair two knotted socks. Have one member put on a blindfold or close their eyes and promise not to peek—"cross your heart and hope to die," as Karl Rohnke says. After the "go" signal, the blindfolded partners try to hit the other team's blindfolded members with the socks like a cannonball shot. The sighted partners give verbal and physical direction to aid in sinking the other "battleships." Once the blindfolded person is hit, or sunk with a sock, the partners switch roles. When both have been hit, they sink into the ocean depths (sit off to the side) exclaiming, "You sank my battleship!"

BRAIN TEASE

Intelligences: Logical/Mathematical, Intrapersonal, Verbal/Linguistic, Interpersonal

Time: 10 min to 15 min (pick one or two to play)

You need: Pen and paper (recommended)

The following sequences to share are sure to make your mind melt into a pool of syrupy grey goo. I'm still trying to get mine back into shape!

Z O T T F F S S E N T

(Answer: The first letter of the word for numbers from zero to ten, i.e., zero, one, two, three, and so on.)

8 5 4 9 1 7 6 3 2 0

(Answer: The numbers are in alphabetical order, according to the first letter of each word, i.e., eight, five, four, and so on.)

D J F M A M J J A S O N

(Answer: These are the first letters of months of the year, i.e., December, January, February, etc.)

Sally Green likes books, but hates to read.

Sally Green likes grass, but hates a lawn.

Sally Green likes business, but hates work.

Sally Green likes bees, but hates honey.

(Answer: Sally Green likes anything with two consecutive letters the same, but hates anything without two consecutive letters the same. Just imagine how she feels about the Mississippi!)

By adding just three lines either horizontally, vertically, or diagonally you will be able to make a "crook in a white house" out of the following pattern of lines:

| | | \ O | |

(Answer: N I X O N)

FUZZY MATH

Intelligences: Bodily/Kinesthetic, Logical/Mathematical, Visual/Spatial, Verbal/Linguistic,

Interpersonal, Intrapersonal, Naturalist

Time: 10 min to 15 min

You need: Bunch of similar objects, e.g., spoons or pens

Place a bunch of similar objects, such as matches, spoons, sticks, pens, etc., in a pattern on a flat surface. The shape you make can look like a chicken, a mess of markers, a "T," anything. After you have finished placing the objects in a pattern, lay your fingers on your knee or beside the pattern. The number of fingers that you lay out on the table is the number the pattern "makes." If you are making a pretend one, you put out one finger. The number is related only to the number of fingers you hold out. As you change the pattern, change the number of fingers you lay out. You can make it from zero to ten easily. Once someone else catches on, you can get from zero to twenty if you want—that really messes people up!

SARDINES

Intelligences: Bodily/Kinesthetic, Visual/Spatial, Verbal/Linguistic, Interpersonal, Naturalist

Time: 10 min to 15 min

You need: Good hiding places

Designate boundaries (inside a building's hallways and stairwells, for example) and ask for a volunteer to hide. Huddle the rest of the group up and have them count to seventy-six. Once they reach seventy-six, everyone shouts at the top of their lungs, "Ready or not, here we come!" Then the group disperses to find the lone sardine, and as they do, they hide along with that person. The game continues until everyone is hiding in the same place together. The last person to find the group is the first person to hide next time.

CROSSED OR UNCROSSED

Intelligences: Bodily/Kinesthetic, Logical/Mathematical, Visual/Spatial, Verbal/Linguistic,

Interpersonal, Naturalist, Intrapersonal

Time: 10 min to 15 min

You need: Two sticks (i.e., pens, spoons, or actual sticks)

You will need two sticks of some sort. Everyone sits in a circle. The team builder starts, holding the two sticks, and says, "I'm passing these sticks crossed," or, "I'm passing these sticks uncrossed." The person receiving the sticks says, "I'm receiving these sticks crossed (or uncrossed), and I'm passing them uncrossed." The terms "crossed" and "uncrossed" actually refer to whether the speaker's *legs* are crossed or uncrossed. Tell the learners whether they are doing it right or wrong and see if they can figure out the pattern.

4. GROUP PURPOSE

HOLE IN ONE

Intelligences: Bodily/Kinesthetic, Logical/Mathematical, Visual/Spatial, Verbal/Linguistic,

Interpersonal, Naturalist

Time: 10 min to 15 min

You need: One soft toy per pair

Invite your group to divide into pairs and give each pair a soft toy. Explain how inspired you are to play golf after your previous dialogue on the subject, so you are going to teach them how to play Toy Store style. Simply have partners take turns as the golfer and catcher. The partners set up their holes and identify them as their mission by picking landmarks. They decide on par ratings for each hole, and each stroke represents something that the individual must do to be successful, which they must identify. For example, that back table is your quarterly sales objective and par is eight strokes—one for each sale I, the golfer, make. One partner is the golfer, while the other partner is the catcher/target. The latter is directed by the golfer as to where to stand and the positioning of goals. For example, the first spot is a sale to Client X.

The catchers catch the toy. A successful catch is defined as the toy going through the arms of the catcher, which are positioned in the shape of an O, and without the catcher moving their feet.

Once the golfers have a successful catch, they move to the position where the catchers are and will continue to shoot from there and identify the next goal, which might be sale to client Y that leads to the predetermined mission. This pattern continues until the golfers make successful shots to the predetermined hole and achieve the mission (i.e., light switch on wall, which is sale to Client X).

Each toss of the soft toy is counted as a stroke, whether or not the toys goes through the O. If the golfer misses the O, they can reposition the catcher if they wish—this is like re-establishing goals. When the pairs make the predetermined hole, they can switch roles and choose a new hole.

MOONBALL

Intelligences: Bodily/Kinesthetic, Logical/Mathematical, Visual/Spatial, Verbal/Linguistic,

Interpersonal, Musical

Time: 10 min to 15 min

You need: Beach ball

For this activity you will need an inflated beach ball. Challenge the group to keep the ball from hitting the ground. The only other rules are that they can use only hands (reduces the risk of people getting kicked—that hurts and hurt isn't fun), and everyone must touch the ball once before anyone can hit it a second time. This way everyone gets to play, and that is fun! If you find they are successful quickly, you can offer to increase the challenge by assigning a number of consecutive group hits; sing a song and everyone must hit the ball before it's over; or deflate the ball a bit.

I LIKE YOU BECAUSE… (BUY IT HERE)

Intelligences: Bodily/Kinesthetic, Verbal/Linguistic, Interpersonal, Naturalist, Musical, Intrapersonal

Time: 10 min

You need: Marker, sheet of paper per person, tape

Participants write, "I like you because …" on the top of their sheet of paper with their marker. Next, have everyone tape their paper to their back. Now, mingle around the room and answer the question by writing your answer (a word or two) on the paper stuck to that person's back. When time is up or everyone has made it to everyone else's back – people can remove and read their paper. *Alternative for super bonded group:* you can do this sitting around a table, too. Have the person to the left of the person on the hot seat write down the answers for that person so they can keep it for later to reflect on it. In this case, people verbally tell that person why they like them. All the person on the hot seat can say is "thank you."

MOONBALL BUDDY ROPE

Intelligences: Bodily/Kinesthetic, Logical/Mathematical, Visual/Spatial, Verbal/Linguistic,

Interpersonal, Musical

Time: 10 min to 15 min

You need: Beach ball, small length of rope per person

Everyone stands in a circle and places at least one foot in a small rope placed on the ground in a circle, a "buddy rope". The additional rule to the classic moonball activity is that participants must maintain contact with the ground inside the buddy rope or they will suffocate because their oxygen line runs up through the bottom of their foot. Classic moonball goals (i.e. most consecutive hits without the ball hitting the ground, or most hits without moving your feet, etc.).

LOOP THE TIE

Intelligences: Bodily/Kinesthetic, Visual/Spatial, Verbal/Linguistic, Interpersonal, Naturalist

Time: 10 min to 15 min

You need: Two ties or hula hoop, stopwatch

Attach two of your ties together to create a closed loop, or use a hula hoop. ("*Pssst!* Wanna buy an *O!*") Then, have your entire group stand "Velcro shoulders" style, holding hands, first placing the looped ties around their wrists so that the loop of the ties is caught up in the loop of the circle. (I just read that twice, it mostly makes sense. I think you'll get the idea.) The challenge for the group is to pass the looped ties clockwise around the circle without letting go of hands. Time how long this takes. You could increase the challenge by having them not talk, close their eyes, continuously whistle until completion, etc. Make up some (beatable) world record and challenge them to do it faster. Have them try again and set incremental goals to reach collective success.

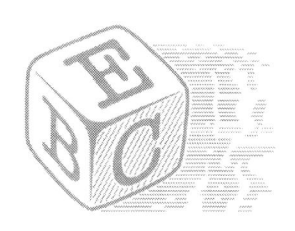

The Piggy Bank: Rewarding, Recognizing, and Appreciating with Intelligence

1. REWARDS

Effort comes before reward.

Brian Offenberger

Those three things—autonomy, complexity, and a connection between effort and reward—are, most people will agree, the three qualities that work has to have if it is to be satisfying.

Malcolm Gladwell

For every disciplined effort there is a multiple reward.

Jim Rohn

Bob Nelson, author of 1001 Ways series, says, "Rewards are not prizes, they are earned gifts." That earned gift can be a smile, a pat on the back, or a new car. The reward should reflect the importance of a specific behaviour or outcome that benefits the group or project. Make sure you have a clearly defined reward system that everyone is aware of so that all employees can work toward achieving it. Your rewards are tools to motivate your group to perform a desired behaviour more often, so make sure that you are consistent and timely in giving them out.

Here are some guidelines to think about when aiming to inspire your work teams to achieve greatness.

1. "You Get What You Reward" - Be on the lookout for employees doing good things. When you see them "doing good," reward and/or appreciate them. Also, let people know well in advance what you are providing as rewards, and be sure to follow through with the reward. For example, when an employee works overtime, send a thank-you card to their partner at home for that extra time commitment.

2. "Nothing Is as Unfair as Equal Treatment of Unequal Performers" - Provide incentive to those who have earned it, not necessarily for everyone all the time. Base your reward on performance, not on whether that person has or has not been rewarded before.

3. "What Motivates People, Motivates People" - What drives people to perform is as unique as their individual Multiple Intelligence Quotient (MIQ). Explore what type of reward an employee would like. Hobbies and interests are a great place to start. For example, maybe one person is a coffee drinker. Give them a personalized coffee mug. Another person enjoys scrapbooking. Give them a new paper punch.

4. "The Best Rewards Often Cost the Least" - The sincere verbal thanks or quick thank-you notes are often the best motivators. It is the thought that counts; however, that thought needs to be expressed at the right time, in the right place, and in the right way for the right person. No pressure, eh?

5. "Everyone Wants to be Appreciated" - People like to feel that what they do is important and valued. Find opportunities to appreciate individually the good job that everyone does in your organization.

6. "Behaviour Is Controlled by Consequences" - If you can provide regular, positive consequences for positive behaviour, you will create more positive behaviour.

7. "Team Spirit Is What You Do with People, not to People" - Involve people in the planning process for your work team. Find out what excites people about being part of your group, what they are proud of, and what they like to do. Then create opportunities for them to be involved in the planning, operation, and evaluation of their favourite parts of the project or organization.

8"Practice Makes Perfect" - What matters is not what you believe or say, it is what you do. Practice providing rewards and appreciation for people's daily, weekly, quarterly, and annual achievements.

WHAT'S DOABLE

Intelligences: Logical/Mathematical, Bodily/Kinesthetic, Naturalist, Musical

Time: 1 hr to 4 hr

You need: Prizes

Not every organization can provide the rewards of its counterparts. That's where you have to start to strengthen the creative bones in your body, and push senior leadership to get on-board. Take a few minutes and think about what behaviours you want to reward: getting to work on time, no sick days, increased sales, etc. Think about things that are measurable, preferably already being tracked, and things you want to encourage.

Next, build a program for your team. Pick your measurable behaviours/results that you want to reward. Set the bars at achievable but not easy levels and within organizational values and expectations. Link a reward to the achievement (e.g., "Here to Win Reward" - Given to the employee who shows up on time for every shift this quarter - $10 Coffee Card). Remember that when you are budgeting, it is possible for everyone to win the reward because they are earned gifts.

LEVEL UP

Intelligences: Interpersonal, Bodily/Kinesthetic, Logical/Mathematical, Verbal/Linguistic, Musical

Time: 1 hr to 4 hr

You need: Prizes

It's time to gamify your work process. Basically, gamification is building a game around a mundane or regular task. Set some rules that are challenging but achievable and track the team's progress. A well-run game will engage and align your team. A poorly designed game will do just the opposite. In your game people will earn badges, prizes, and bragging rights as they achieve levels. You will set up ahead of time how team members individually and collectively achieve those levels.

Find a task (or series of tasks) that you want to encourage. Build your game rules around those tasks. For example, if you want to encourage learning of leadership skills, make available an enrolment into an online leadership development program for each of your team. Set a "ladder" style badge reward structure for course module completion. Have the green button "in it" badge given to each person who signs up and completes their first course module. Then have the orange button "on it" badge given to the member who completes five modules. Following that, you could get the blue button "working it" badge to give to the person who has completed ten modules. And finally, the gold "mastered it" badge to the person who completes all twenty modules in the program. With achieving the gold badge, the team member receives a $100 gift card to a local restaurant.

COACHING

Intelligences: Intrapersonal, Bodily/Kinesthetic, Logical/Mathematical, Musical

Time: 1 hr to 4 hr

You need: Prizes

The value of performance appraisals is the practice of team members setting and achieving professional goals (and sometimes personal, too, depending on the company). The gap is often how they are incentivized, coached, and managed along the way. If you attach a "reward" to the achievement of the goal, you will help to improve the bench strength of your team.

Establish a set "reward" that you can afford to invest in each of your team members should they all achieve their performance goals (e.g., $50 prepaid credit card, or a "toy" that relates to their hobby). Next, during your performance appraisal meeting with your team member, have them establish a goal that they want to achieve this year. Take your time, making sure it is a SMART goal and challenging. Next, have them establish a reward that would make achieving this goal worthwhile, given your monetary, time, or other constraints. Once the team member has established their goal, document the goal and the reward. As a team, have the members share their goals with the team. Coach the team members toward their goals—with the hope that everyone will achieve their reward. Give the rewards as goals are achieved, that way the rewarding of one might be incentive to another member to revisit and re-energize toward goal attainment.

2. RECOGNITION

Don't work for recognition, but do work worthy of recognition.

H. Jackson Brown Jr.

Research indicates that workers have three prime needs: interesting work, recognition for doing a good job, and being let in on things that are going on in the company.

Zig Ziglar

People work for money but go the extra mile for recognition, praise, and rewards.

Dale Carnegie

One of the most powerful tools for increasing team and individual engagement is recognition from a manager, senior leader, and peers. When someone goes above and beyond or does quality work in some way, it is vital that you recognize those efforts. These recognitions need not break the bank. However, they do need to be timely and specific. They need to be timely in that you need to catch the employee as early as possible upon their completion of the task. This shows that you are attentive and interested in their work (and the work of the team). You need to specifically indicate what you are recognizing them for. This demonstrates your authenticity and understanding of the work that they do.

There are abundant ways to recognize an employee, but the most powerful are an immediate verbal recognition/thank you and/or a handwritten note of recognition. Both are free of cost, other than your time and caring.

COFFEE UP

Intelligences: Interpersonal, Verbal/Linguistic, Visual/Spatial

Time: 30 min to 2 hr

You need: Paper, pen/pencil, coffee

Want to recognize an employee but do not have much budget? Help them coffee up. Let's take an employee who goes above and beyond at their job. You want to recognize them for their extra effort. Often, new employees or other upwardly mobile employees want to gain attention to help with their promotion desires.

You can help them by linking them to your network. This can be done in several ways. One is at a senior leadership meeting, publicly make note of this team member at your meeting table. Then, after the meeting send an email to your senior leader, asking them to send a quick handwritten note to that employee for the extra work they did. Another thing you can arrange is a coffee meeting with that same senior leader and the employee themselves. This gives the employee some face-to-face time with the senior leader.

BIG BANG, NO BUDGET

Intelligences: All depending on the solution chosen

Time: 20 min to 4 hr

You need: Will depend on the solution chosen

Who's kidding who, budgets are tight. Sometimes, it feels like they are the only metric that matters (*sigh*). But even with tight budgets, leaders can recognize their team and its members for the work they are doing. Here are some low- and medium-cost recognition ideas:

- √ Get them a fresh cup of tea or coffee for their break.
- √ Write a note about why they went above and beyond and give it to their senior leader.
- √ Get them a new fancy pen.
- √ Get them a new lanyard for their key card with "thank you" written on it.
- √ Bake a cake or cookies.
- √ Get them an inexpensive gift card for coffee.
- √ Write an article about them in the staff newsletter.
- √ Appoint them to a staff council or project group.
- √ Buy them a small gift that relates to a hobby they have.
- √ Write them a thank-you note.
- √ Get them a bottle of mineral water.
- √ Get them a coupon for something you can do for them.
- √ Get them a new book.

CIRCLE OF INFLUENCE

Intelligences: Interpersonal, Bodily/Kinesthetic, Visual/Spatial, Naturalist, Verbal/Linguistic

Time: 20 min

You need: Markers, sticky labels

Peer-to-peer recognition is a great avenue to fuel up your team. Making real effort to make this a habit is easier than you think. Here's how: at the beginning of each meeting have everyone get a partner. Ask them to think about one thing that they have seen their partner do since the last meeting that they think should be recognized. Give them some examples of things you have seen by calling out team members in the room for their specific accomplishments. Then go around the room and have each person share the recognition of their partner. You can up the impact by giving each person a sticky label and have them make a "recognition badge." Tell your team that this is going to be a part of the regular meeting structure, so to keep an eye out for people's accomplishments.

HALT ENTITLED RECOGNITIONS

Intelligences: All depending on the solution chosen

Time: 20 min to 4 hr

You need: Depends on solution chosen

What is expected is no longer a recognition or reward—it's an expectation. Take some time to rethink how you are recognizing and rewarding your teams. Are there things that have become expectations? If so you might consider weaning your team off of those. Do so by slowly removing expected things and adding more unexpected recognitions. This won't work if the balance is tipped. So be sure to logically add and delete simultaneously—and be wary of cultural expectations (you might just have to keep those). Try adding some different recognitions. Here are some ideas:

- Get employee to demonstrate something they do very well to the team or management.

- Say "thank you."

- Give them a handwritten note of thanks.

- Help employees access professional development opportunities.

- Give employees the opportunity to share their new skill or innovation with upper management.

- Allow employees to pick their next assignments.

- Acknowledge at meetings other "achievements" staff have obtained, such as "4H volunteer of the year" or "a new granddaughter."

- Put a letter of praise in the employee's file.

- Send a birthday card.

- Increase your "motivation vocabulary," and use it more often (e.g., excellent, superbly done, awesome, etc.)

IT'S A GROUP THING

Intelligences: All depending on solution chosen

Time: 20 min to 4 hr

You need: Will depend on the solution chosen

A random surprise is always the best. Make a meeting reminder in your calendar to find a thing to recognize your team for each month. To keep it "random," don't make it every second Tuesday, or always a tray of fancy coffees. Mix it up. A great way to do that is to tie it sometimes to special events (i.e., Halloween, Valentine's Day) or special industry times (i.e., budget approval, occupational health and safety week). Find a simple way to recognize your team for the work they did in respect to your established goals, behaviours, vision, etc. Here are some easy ideas to implement group recognitions:

- Bring in a snack tray to thank your team.
- Take action on issues that staff bring to your attention and follow up with them.
- Have a tailgate barbecue (bring your barbecue or bring in some food trucks).
- Set up an ice cream bar on a hot day.
- Provide a yoga or other desired class.
- Get team T-shirts/sweatshirts done to recognize an achievement.
- Take your team minigolfing.
- Give massage certificates "in recognition of achieving __."
- Upgrade the staff lounge by adding a sofa, new paint, etc., with a plaque identifying the team recognition.

3. APPRECIATION

A person who feels appreciated will always do more than what is expected.

Unknown

Appreciation is a wonderful thing: it makes what is excellent in others belong to us as well.

Voltaire

Appreciation can make a day, even change a life. Your willingness to put it into words is all that is necessary.

Margaret Cousins

This is the piece of employee empowerment that you can give very generously. Walking around businesses and connecting with staff is the number one thing that employees seek from their manager/leader. Being seen by your employees is key, but taking a moment to acknowledge and appreciate their contributions is the jet fuel that propels the ship.

Appreciation is the authentic acknowledgement of effort that employees put into their work. This can come in many forms, but honestly, need not be expensive, lavish, or a showstopper. The really powerful appreciations are simple, timely, and authentic expressions by a manager to an employee. From a simple verbal thank you to a handwritten note, these become your tools that will solidify and enhance employee engagement.

Appreciation is given continually to the group members for any task that supports the group success. Usually, appreciation is verbal recognition to an individual or group, which acknowledges that what they have done immediately benefits the project's success. It needs to be a conscious quest for the leader in the beginning. Eventually, expressing appreciation will become a habit for you, and it will foster a positive work environment for your employees.

Some Appreciative Terms

- Thank you for ____.

- The ____ you did looks great.

- Great job with ____.

- Top-notch work on ____.

- Your speed is equalled by quality in ____.

- Amazing work with ____.

- I'm impressed by your ____.

- I heard someone say ____ about you. Well done!

- You never cease to amaze me with things like ____.

- Wow, you outdid yourself with ____.

TEN COINS

Intelligences: All

Time: 20 min to 1 hr

You need: Ten coins

What is recognized is repeated. The trick for good managers is to build a behaviour that has them mindful of the work their employees are doing, and consistently and authentically acknowledging them for it.

One thing you can do is place ten coins in your right-hand pocket. Throughout the day, work toward moving the collection of coins to your left pocket. Here is the only rule for this game: you need to authentically appreciate someone. After you have done that you can move one coin from the right to left pocket. An appreciation can be in the form of a handwritten note, a verbal thank you, an acknowledgement for added effort/thought/action, etc. Your challenge as manager is to be on the lookout to identify ten in the course of the day.

MOBILE CAR WASH

Intelligences: Interpersonal, Bodily/Kinesthetic, Visual/Spatial, Verbal/Linguistic

Time: 20 min

You need: Cars, washing supplies, note paper, pens, envelopes

A quick surprise on a Friday is great way to appreciate your staff. There are lots of quick appreciations you can do, too. Remember that your appreciation is simple, timely, and authentic.

If you have a bit of a budget and can bring in a mobile car wash (or hire a local school/service group looking for a fundraiser) to set up in your parking lot, invite your team to bring their cars over and have them washed for the weekend. Leave a handwritten note in an envelope under their windshield wiper, thanking them for their help and great work.

REAL FACE BOOK

Intelligences: Interpersonal, Visual/Spatial, Intrapersonal, Verbal/Linguistic

Time: 20 min

You need: Online photobook maker, photos

Creating an appreciation for a team milestone is important. It could represent the end of a fiscal period or completion of a project. No matter what the celebration is, a thoughtful and real appreciation gift can truly make a difference. Here's an idea of an appreciation you can build that will hopefully see your employees sharing their success with their family and friends.

Take photos of your team, with permission, at a retreat, on the job, from their past, etc., and compile a photo book that celebrates a milestone. Include some data about each team member, such as where they are from, what they do for the company, and even quirky things (stay away from inside jokes, instead keep to the empowering/thankful messaging). You can grab this information by sending out a quick "survey" before you start putting the book together. These are particularly good for teams working virtually.

I LIKE YOU BECAUSE...

Intelligences: Interpersonal, Bodily/Kinesthetic, Visual/Spatial, Verbal/Linguistic

Time: 10 min to 20 min

You need: Paper, markers

Building a culture of appreciation means making it part of the day-to-day. Appreciation need not be something that employees look for just from you. Instead, build a culture that encourages your team members to appreciate each other. Giving positive feedback should become a cultural thing. Here is a quick activity you can do at a meeting, pot luck, etc.

Write "I like you because..." on the top of a piece of paper and photocopy enough for everyone in your team. Tape the paper on the backs of every person in your team. Pass out some markers and have people move from person to person, answering the statement about why they like each individual. At the end of the allotted time, have the team members remove their papers from their backs. Remind your team that it's these compliments that shouldn't be kept to oneself but rather shared. It is the authentic appreciation of each other that helps us to become a great team.

Debriefing: Learning with Intelligence

PAPER AIRPLANES

Intelligences: Bodily/Kinesthetic, Intrapersonal, Interpersonal

Time: 10 min to 20 min

You need: Pens, crayons, pencils/markers, paper

Pass out materials to each learner and ask them to write something important about themselves, such as an exciting past event in their life, a goal they have, a lifestyle they desire, a behaviour they wish to stop, or learning from a past event. Fold the paper into an airplane. Either toss the paper within the circle to share with other learners, or, if the theme is something they would like to discard, throw the paper airplanes off a cliff, into a campfire, etc., to metaphorically get rid of what's on the paper. You can do a similar activity with rocks by visualizing something you wish to discard (such as rage) and tossing the rock into the ocean or a lake saying, "It is done!"

GROUP BANNER

Intelligences: Visual/Spatial, Bodily/Kinesthetic, Logical/Mathematical, Interpersonal

Time: 20 min to 30 min

You need: Craft materials (markers, paint, etc.), bedsheet or large sheet of paper

The group will become one collective Picasso to create a banner that expresses who they are. They can express facets of their group, such as things they do to be effective, things that bug them, or individual things such as I like…, I want the group to know…, etc. It is up to you to decide how the banner will fit into your productive process. Display the banner. This is an excellent group behaviour contracting tool because it can be displayed and easily referred to when necessary.

WHAT I'VE BECOME!

Intelligences: Interpersonal, Intrapersonal, Logical/Mathematical, Verbal/Linguistic

Time: 20 min

You need: Pens/pencils, paper

Pass out pens and paper to each learner. Have them spend some time thinking or talking with a partner about all the things they want to achieve in their lives. Then have each learner write their obituary that will include their most important accomplishments. To aid them in conceptualizing the activity, read them an obituary that you have created for yourself ahead of time. This is a good end-of-the-day activity for a group or to use as a debrief for goal setting, visioning, or mission statements.

BUILDING BLOCKS

Intelligences: Verbal/Linguistic, Bodily/Kinesthetic, Interpersonal, Intrapersonal

Time: 10 min to 20 min

You need: Building blocks with pictures or letters, cloth bag

Pass around the bag of blocks while the group sits in a circle, inviting each learner to remove a block. Ask them to think of a word that starts with the letter on the block or has something to do with the picture on the block. Do a whip around the circle. Each learner will start by showing their block and presenting their word. They will then discuss how that word applies to their learning achieved through the experience. You can probe their learning from there.

This is a great tool because it gives everyone something to hold while they speak. A quick and dirty tool for debriefing that is fun.

MESSAGE IN A BOTTLE

Intelligences: Verbal/Linguistic, Bodily/Kinesthetic, Interpersonal, Musical—depending on the message

Time: 30 min

You need: Lake, bottle with a cork (or a water bottle),

Note: Write a note inviting participants on an adventure or to deliver an evening thought.

The trick is to write the message and get it in the water without the participants seeing you. The application is up to you. I used it once with a map and a list of instructions to bring a group of young people to a lecture. It can be a tool to offer a mysterious observation of group functioning or an introduction to an activity—this can be used as either a briefing or debriefing activity.

BUSINESS CARDS

Intelligences: Interpersonal, Verbal/Linguistic, Visual/Spatial, Logical/Mathematical

Time: 10 min to 20 min

You need: A personal business card from each individual

Have each learner supply one of their business cards to the facilitator. Use the blank side of the card for group members to write feedback to the individual who owns the card, such as their most enduring quality, best contribution to the group, best asset, etc., as per the program objectives. Return cards to their rightful owners. This is an excellent post-program reminder of learning derived from the program. This is an easy way for corporate clients to learn to provide positive feedback without being judged by co-workers or the recipient.

SIDEWALK CHALK

Intelligences: Visual/Spatial, Intrapersonal, Verbal/Linguistic, Interpersonal

Time: 20 min to 30 min

You need: Sidewalk or tarmac, sidewalk chalk

Distribute sidewalk chalk to learners either as individuals, pairs, or small groups. Have the learners draw on the sidewalk an image that represents how they feel or what they learned during an initiative. Have learners describe their sidewalk mural to the group. Use the mural to construct questions that are appropriate to the individual's learning needs. This activity is fun, colourful, inexpensive, and easy.

BLINDFOLDED DEBRIEF

Intelligences: Verbal/Linguistic, Visual/Spatial, Interpersonal

Time: 10 min to 30 min

You need: One blindfold per learner

Provide learners with blindfolds, unless they are still wearing them from a previous activity. Have the learners wear the blindfolds during the debrief. This will compel them to respect one another's right to speak, create a speaking order, listen more closely, and avoid distractions. Remove the blindfolds when the debrief is over or their function is achieved. Great activity, but be careful—some people may find being blindfolded downright scary, and that's not good.

DYADIC ENCOUNTER

Intelligences: Verbal/Linguistic, Intrapersonal, Interpersonal, Logical/Mathematical

Time: 20 min

You need: Pre-made dyadic booklets

Divide your group into pairs. Give each pair a copy of the dyadic booklet. Establish a place to meet once they have completed the exercise or time has run out. Each pair finds a secluded place to complete the encounter. Each person will have an opportunity to respond to the open-ended statements in the booklet prior to moving on to the next one. Organize your statements in a progression to achieve the learning outcomes you desire. This experience is effective for getting the most people talking about the same subjects in the same order. It is a great way to generate and share many perspectives on the same topic.

ANSWERS IN A HAT

Intelligences: Bodily/Kinesthetic, Linguistic, Visual/Spatial, Intrapersonal

Time: 10 min to 30 min

You need: Paper, pens/pencils, hat, two chairs

Have each learner write down on a sheet of paper an issue (problem) that they are concerned about and then fold it. Collect the folded sheets in a hat. Have the group sit in a semi-circle facing two chairs. Have a volunteer (or selected learner) sit in one of the chairs and read an issue from the hat. Learners then provide feedback on the issue by perhaps suggesting how they would solve it. The second chair is an "open seat" where another learner can sit to provide their two cents' worth. When someone sits on the second seat, the person in the first seat must leave and take a place in the semi-circle. The trading of seats continues until everyone has had their adequate say on the topic. This exercise provides options and suggestions on how to solve an issue for at least one individual in a group. It can also be used to discuss issues within the group such as behavioural conflicts or other management concerns.

JAR OF INQUIRY

Intelligences: Visual/Spatial, Verbal/Linguistic, Interpersonal, Logical/Mathematical

Time: 10 min to 1 hr

You need: Large, clean, empty pickle jar, scrap paper, pencil, decoration materials

Talk with the group about how questions are sometimes hard to ask publicly. Invite learners to help decorate the Jar of Inquiry. Tell them to feel free to write any questions on the paper provided and put them in the jar. On a regular basis, at lunch for example, answer or facilitate a discussion around the questions in the jar. This is especially effective for groups who need to ask questions but are not necessarily comfortable with those individuals they need to ask the questions of. As a manager, you can pad the jar with questions that you feel the group needs to discuss. This is a great activity that can be run continuously with a group.

JOURNAL

Intelligences: All depending on application

Time: Varies

You need: One journal per learner, pens/pencils

Pass out a journal to each learner. Provide them with open-ended statements, quotes, questions, pictures, magazine ads, etc., to be placed in their journals. Ask the learners to respond to the entries that you have provided. Invite them to write free-form. Use as an evaluative tool or personal progress log for the learner. This activity is a nice addition to a long-term program and a different way to provide continuous feedback to employees instead of the dreaded (and ineffective) performance review. Provides excellent growth opportunities, but does take some time.

DIALOGUE JOURNAL

Intelligences: All depending on application

Time: Varies

You need: One journal per learner, pens/pencils

Pass out a journal to each learner. Provide time within your program or business day for learners to write in their journals. You can either structure the entries with open-ended statements or direct questions. As well, unstructured entries (blank sheets of paper) can be effective. Make sure learners understand that only the two of you will read these entries. After learners have completed their entry, have them pass the journals back to you. Respond to their questions, make suggestions, and provide support to learners. This is effective with groups you work with long term. It helps learners who are uncomfortable asking questions in the group. In addition, you can readily measure program feedback, evaluation, and group readiness. The books can be passed on to other group members for comment as well, if the group agrees that's okay. Be careful to guard the privacy of the previous writings in the journals.

POLAROID MOMENTS

Intelligences: Visual/Spatial, Logical/Mathematical, Interpersonal

Time: 20 min

You need: Polaroid instant camera (or digital camera), film

Use an instant camera to photograph the group involved in learning activities or day-to-day work. Photos can be put in an album and mailed back to the group post-program, creatively displayed in your office space, or used in a slide show to spur discussion. You can designate a "staff photographer" from the group on a day-to-day or hour-to-hour basis, take the photos yourself, or offer each person in your group an hour to take pictures related to a certain subject. This is an excellent reflective tool, great to use during an initiative task or on its own to generate discussion. It can be used as a memory device for group achievements, to discuss specific moments during an initiative, or to identify specific issues. Caution: This can be a costly option. Digital cameras can make this marginally more cost-effective!

T-SHIRT PAINTING

Intelligences: Visual/Spatial, Interpersonal, Intrapersonal, Bodily/Kinesthetic

Time: 20 min to 1 hr

You need: T-shirts (one per learner), paint, fabric medium writing tools, paint brushes, iron

T-shirts can be used in a variety of ways as a processing tool—the possibilities are as varied as your imagination. For example, print your objectives on the shirt and check them off as you complete them. Have group members write reasons they like a person on the back of that person's shirt. After each learning experience, have learners paint a symbol, picture, or word that represents what they learned or derived from that activity. It can be costly, but it sure is fun.

POSTCARDS FROM PARADISE

Intelligences: Visual/Spatial, /Verbal/Linguistic, Interpersonal, Logical/Mathematical

Time: 20 min

You need: Postcards bought or made by learners

Have each learner write a "postcard from paradise" to someone within the group or outside it about the experience they just had or one you'd like to talk about (e.g., an initiative task, staff accolade, or idea for improvement). Have learners share their postcards to initiate productive processing. As well, you can have your group write down on postcards commitments to improvement they have made during the meeting, self-address them, and then collect them to mail after the session.

SUN, CLOUDS, RAIN

Intelligences: Visual/Spatial, Bodily/Kinesthetic, Interpersonal

Time: 5 min

You need: No specific props required for this processing tool

Set a scale for learners to indicate how they are feeling: sun (lovin' it), clouds (okay), or rain (not so good). Have learners stand by the icon or spot that represents best how they are feeling. You could use this tool to gather information concerning the program, learners' readiness for physical activity, their comfort level, meal enjoyment, and much more! This is a quick evaluation tool that can be applied to get a representative sample of your group.

PLAY DOUGH SCULPTING

Intelligences: Visual/Spatial, Verbal/Linguistic, Interpersonal

Time: 20 min

You need: Clay or Fimo and associated tools, or play dough or cookie dough

Pass out play dough (or other sculpting material) to learners. Ask them to make a sculpture to represent some aspect of your debrief. Learners may trade, keep, or eat their sculpture (if it's edible, of course). To extend the experience, create a unified sculpture to represent the group's collective learning outcomes. It's fun in the forming stages of group development to have people make things that represent them.

SLIDE SHOW

Intelligences: Visual/Spatial, Interpersonal, Logical/Mathematical, Musical

Time: 20 min

You need: Light switch that controls room lights (or a big flashlight outside at night); or digital camera, screen, PowerPoint, and projector

Break into small groups. Have learners briefly discuss the experience they just had. Instruct them to use their entire small group to create five scenes (or slides) that were the "best parts of the trip," for example. Have each group act out their scene, with narration, while the other groups watch the show. Turn the lights out while they set the first slide. Turn them on for a couple of seconds and then off while the group sets up the next slide, and so on, until they are finished their slides. It's a fun debrief. As well, a nice touch can be added with popcorn, a cartoon in the beginning, ushers, or anything else to evoke a theatre experience.

SPEAKER'S STICK

Intelligences: Verbal/Linguistic, Bodily/Kinesthetic, Interpersonal, Intrapersonal

Time: 10 min to 1 hr

You need: Ceremonial stick (the group can create this by attaching to the stick something important to them)

Use the stick to manage who is speaking within the group (i.e., whoever holds the stick is the only one allowed to speak). No stick, no speak. Not hard. (There is a traditional First Nations ceremony called a Talking Circle on which this entry is based. Contact a local First Nations band leader for a more in-depth look at this beautiful and powerful ceremony.) This is an effective tool for those facilitators who find their group is unmanageable when it comes to speaking out during the debrief. Note: The facilitator must respect the stick equally with the learners to maintain legitimacy of the stick's significance.

TALK CROSS TALK

Intelligences: Interpersonal, Verbal/Linguistic, Bodily/Kinesthetic

Time: 10 min to 1 hr

You need: No specific props required for this processing tool

Divide the group into pairs and have them spread out. Provide the pairs with a topic to talk about. Each person gets an established time (2 minutes) to talk non-stop and uninterrupted. Their partner simply listens, and when the established time is up, they are given a few moments (1 minute) to discuss what they heard. The people in the dyads exchange roles—the talker becomes the listener and vice versa—to perform the above task. This activity is excellent for the facilitator if a learner is disruptive and a group confrontation is not appropriate. Recreationally, it's a great way to get to know people. For the purposes of training and development, it provides great executive summaries of the event for a more in-depth and speedy debrief.

WASHABLE TATTOO

Intelligences: Visual/Spatial, Interpersonal, Intrapersonal

Time: 10 min to 30 min

You need: Washable markers

Give each learner a washable marker. Ask learners to make a tattoo that best represents how they are feeling, something they learned, etc., as a result of the preceding experience or topic. Caution: Use body parts that all learners will be comfortable showing. This activity is great for groups that are comfortable with touch behaviours because you can also have participants draw symbols on other learners that represent that person (e.g., this person is special because…, I value you because…).

RETRO VCR

Intelligences: Logical/Mathematical, Verbal/Linguistic, Interpersonal

Time: 10 min

You need: No specific props required for this processing tool

Ask learners to take a make-believe videotape in their hands. The videotape they hold is like a home video of their experience. Learners can press pause, play, and stop. Ask for a volunteer to put the tape in the imaginary VCR and press play. Their job is to narrate what they see happening on the imaginary TV screen. If another individual wants to interject, they can press pause and then continue with the narration. This is an excellent tool to begin reflecting on what has just happened in the experience.

THE WHIP

Intelligences: Interpersonal, Verbal/Linguistic

Time: 10 min to 20 min

You need: No specific props required for this processing tool

Have the group arrange themselves in a circle "Velcro shoulders or knees" style. Ask each learner to complete one specific task or answer a specific question. For example, you could ask, "In one word, what is your greatest strength?" or, "On a scale of zero to ten, how challenged were you by the initiative?" Everyone answers the question, one at a time, as you go around the circle. Jot notes to yourself about how people are responding (both verbally and non-verbally) to your questions. This facilitation tool will provide a plethora of information to an observant and attentive facilitator. It is an excellent way of beginning and/or ending a session. As a beginning, it provides information that can be probed deeper later on with the group, and as a closing it provides a great "feeling check."

LETTER TO YOURSELF

Intelligences: Intrapersonal, Bodily/Kinesthetic, Logical/Mathematical

Time: 10 min to 30 min

You need: Pens, paper, envelopes, sufficient postage for each letter

Pass out the materials required to each participant. Instruct them to write a letter to themselves about the experience they just had. For example, you could have a management group write a letter to themselves about innovative motivational techniques that they want to implement with their work team. Discuss the content of the letters within your group. Collect the letters after the individuals have self-addressed them and mail the letters after the session. This is an effective means of helping learners relive what they learned from the session you provided.

ROAD MAPPING

Intelligences: Logical/Mathematical, Interpersonal, Visual/Spatial

Time: 20 min to 2 hr

You need: Paper, crayons

Have learners create a map of the sequence of activities or events that took place in the learning session. Include where things such as stop signs, traffic lights, turn-offs, destinations, etc., occur on the map. Have learners discuss what they learned metaphorically, in relation to the map. Ask them to become cartographers to make changes to the map or engineers and construction workers to make structural changes to how the roads work. This is a great tool to refer back to occasionally to plan and track a group's development. Also, if the maps are done individually and collectively, it will help people understand the constraints of others in the group.

JUST A NOTE TO SAY

Intelligences: Interpersonal, Visual/Spatial, Verbal/Linguistic, Bodily/Kinesthetic

Time: 20 min

You need: Paper cut in business card-size pieces, pencils/pens, hat or jar

Pass around paper and pens to each learner. Ask them to write a note that you can use to start your debrief. To help them out, ask learners to answer an open-ended question that you pose. Collect the papers in a hat or jar and use them as starting points to spur dialogue. This is a great tool that enables quieter learners to provide direction for the debrief session. You can either discuss them one at a time or read them all at the beginning, but it is important that everyone's note is heard (if not discussed).

RADIO NETWORK

Intelligences: Musical, Bodily/Kinesthetic, Intrapersonal

Time: 30 min to 1 hr

You need: Music, music player, various instruments

Have learners bring some of their favourite music to the session. Prior to the session, ask learners to think about the experience in terms of an expression of lyrics, rhythm, etc., that they are familiar with and that their musical selections contain. Post-experience, have learners choose and share a sound bite of their choice that fits with the experience. This is useful for creating a memory device that the learners will encounter post-session and that supports their long-term ability to reinforce the learning.

BETTY CROCKER'S DEBRIEF

Intelligences: Visual/Spatial, Bodily/Kinesthetic, Interpersonal

Time: 30 min to 1 hr

You need: Box of cake mix and any additional ingredients it calls for, cake pan, oven, paper, pencil/pen, plastic eggs

Prepare open-ended debrief questions on pieces of paper that are pertinent to your group's experience. Package these statements in plastic eggs. Bake the cake in the cake pan according to box's directions. Then put the debrief questions in the baking pan so that when you cut the cake, everyone in your group will get one plastic egg with their serving. Have your group get into dyads or small groups, and then have learners dialogue about the open-ended questions in the eggs while they eat their cake. This is a fun way to reflect on the entire day's activities and learning. It is also a great way to integrate learning into your meals, but it is time-consuming.

TESTIMONIALS

"Tyler Hayden has provided excellent tips and resources for effective team building and stakeholder management in a highly competitive and rapidly changing business climate. This book is a must-read for project leaders, managers, and team members. Readers will find creative and practical advice on every page."

— **Vijay K. Verma, PMI Fellow, PMP, MBA** Organizing Projects for Success; Human Resource Skills for the Project Manager, Managing the Project Team; & *The Art of Positive Politics: A Key to Delivering Successful Projects*

"Tyler has the amazing ability to write a book that pulls at the heartstrings while teaching valuable project management and leadership lessons. For him to then give away some of his tricks of the trade with sharing his exercises and games is just a cherry on top. As a Licensed Engineer, PMP certified, and a Project Management Blogger, my job requires me to plan and coordinate team building for various corporate events. This book is a great way to not only get reinvigorated in my team-building efforts but also a tool to plan an entire training program!"

— **Graham S. M. Briggs, PE, PMP**

"I love the way Tyler has applied Multiple Intelligences to help leaders choose team building tools. It gives them a measurable way to focus team building efforts - creating greater success for leaders and their teams alike."

— **Vince Poscente**, NY Times Bestselling Author of *The Age of Speed*

"Tyler's done an outstanding job of providing a delightfully entertaining and well written book jammed packed with lots of practical tools and applications. That's an extremely rare combination. Highly recommended."

— **Jim Clemmer** international bestselling leadership author *Growing the Distance and Firing on All Cylinders*, speaker, and workshop/retreat facilitator.

"Tyler's book *"The Business That Care About People"* is a brilliant roadmap on how you can build trust and create connections in your organization. With an opening story that captures you and keeps you engaged, Tyler goes on to explain how you can identify each of the multiple intelligences in the people you lead and how you can create more trust with each of them. Because of this book, I now have a great toolbox of activities and ideas that I can use to make my presentations better. If you are really serious about building better teams and creating true connections with others than you'll love this book."

— **Lea Brovedani**, 2017-2019 Trust Across America Top Thought Leader in *"Trust"*. Lea is the author of *Trust Me* and *Trusted*.

"There are lots of books on leadership and team building, and sometimes they are interesting. This book is more than interesting. It's actually useful. Packed with 'how-to' ideas and strategies, it's a must for effective leadership."

— **Joe Calloway**, author, *The Leadership Mindset*

"Tyler's Book is packed with literally hundreds of ideas for you to engage the diverse intelligences that make up your team. You want to be a gold medal manager and leader of teams? Read this book!

— **Adam Kreek**, Author, Executive Coach, Olympic Gold Medalist

Team Building Activities

Join us at www.teambuildingactivities.com and discover Team-Building Activities for leaders who care about their teams.

TeamBuildingActivities.com makes team building easy. Start by signing up for our newsletter so you can stay current as we launch new activities and tools to help you lead rock star team-building activities. As a thank you, we will immediately direct you to a download page where you can access your first activity, a gift from us.

You'll see how easy it is to gain access to team tools that will save you time and improve team engagement and development. By becoming part of our tribe we will help you to reach your team in new and fun ways that are developmentally targeted. You'll be able to simply download activities to your device, follow our simple step-by-step instructions, and our professionally designed team-building activities will ignite your team's connectivity.

Join us to begin your successful implementation of team-building learning products, game packages, books, and much, much more.

REFERENCES

This book is a culmination of years of experience in designing and delivering exciting debriefing/team-building programs. I did not directly reference any of the activities in this book, as I am unsure of their exact origin in a lot of cases. Many come from colleagues in the field, while others come from my own trial and error.

Butler, Steve, and Karl Rohnke. *Quicksilver: Adventure Games, Initiative Problems, Trust Activities and a Guide to Effective Leadership.* Dubuque: Kendall Hunt Publishing, 1995.

Collins, J. C. *Good to Great: Why Some Companies Make the Leap ... and Others Don't.* New York: HarperBusiness, 2001.

Gardner, Howard. *Frames of Mind: The Theory of Multiple Intelligences.* New York: BasicBooks, 1993.

Gass, Michael A. Book of Metaphors, Volume 2. Dubuque: Kendall Hunt Publishing, 1995.

Gawain, Shakti. *Creative Visualization: Use the Power of Your Imagination to Create What You Want in Your Life.* California: New World Library, 1991.

HBR's 10 Must Reads on Leadership. Boston: Harvard Business Review Press, 2011.

HBR's 10 Must Reads on Teams. Boston: Harvard Business Review Press, 2013.

Hunt, Jasper. *Ethical Issues in Experiential Education.* Dubuque:

Kendall Hunt Publishing, 1994.

Kaye, Beverly, and Sharon Jordan-Evans. *Love 'em or Lose 'em: Getting Good People to Stay*. San Francisco: Berrett-Koehler Publishers, 2005.

Lavoie, Rick. "When the Chips Are Down." *YouTube,* speaker Rick Lavoie, May 22, 2014, https://www.youtube.com/watch?v=nApu7fjmLcc.

Nelson, Bob. *1001 Ways to Reward Employees*. New York: Workman Publishing, 1994.

Priest, Simon, and Michael Gass. . *Effective Leadership in Adventure Programming*. Windsor, ON: Human Kinetics, 1997.

Rohnke, Karl. *Silver Bullets: A Guide to Initiative Problems, Adventure Games, and Trust Activities*. Dubuque: Kendall Hunt Publishing, 1984.

———. *Cowstails and Cobras II: A Guide to Games, Initiatives, Ropes Courses, & Adventure Curriculum*. Dubuque: Kendall Hunt Publishing, 1989.

Turner, Suzanne. *The Little Black Book of Management*. New York: McGraw Hill, 2010.

The general model of Experiential Education as suggested by Kolb (1984)

LAST WORD

There is one thing I know. I didn't get here by myself. So, this book, in addition to serving as a tool for project managers and leaders to help build their teams, is also a sort of homage to some of those folks who have helped me out so much.

I wish I could have included everyone, but alas there are only so many characters in the book, and the list of those who have helped, well it's as long as I am tall. So, I chose a few people who fit characters and included them in this book: from my daughters, Tait and Breton, to my mom, Sandy, and dad, Granddad, to the main character, John.

I want to tell you a bit about John. He was my teacher for grades 7 and 8, a dad, and a loving husband. When he inherited me in his class I was (and still am) a ball of energy. Me as a young student is not something I'd wish on any educator. Coupled with high energy, I came in with what would now be diagnosed as learning disabilities. In fact, I was in remedial education for a speech impediment and needed extra help in all the core subjects. In grade 6 my teachers labelled me a bunch of things that pigeon-holed me.

Then, enter John Gaynor.

He sat with me. He helped me with my spelling, math, and behaviour. He told me that I didn't need remedial education. He suggested that in fact I needed enrichment education (aka the "smart" kids' programs). He told me that I was just really smart in different ways and not challenged with the traditional ways that people learned. So off I went to public speaking events, classes about the stock market, young inventor's workshops, National Geographic acid rain studies, and creative writing workshops.

I don't think Mr. Gaynor had read Howard Gardner's *Frames of Mind* that details how learners have different strengths in the ways they learn. But, somehow Mr. Gaynor recognized mine. In doing so he opened me up to become a productive and successful student because I knew what I could do, and do well. I utilized my strengths to benefit my workload and the workloads of my teams.

This book showcases him in name because he was someone who believed in me. We've all had those people in our lives. Pause now and thank them if you can—make a call, send an email, do something. Then, pay it forward by reading this book and applying how you can be that person in other people's lives—particularly the teams you manage.

Livin' Life Large, my motto, is about passionately living every single moment of every single day. Our ability to give back to others through great management and leadership is a gift that we can share. To that end, this book is intended to share with you the central tool I have been using as a team designer for the last two decades. I look forward to reading a book where you are a character like John.

This is John Gaynor I'm thankful our paths crossed.

Tyler Hayden is a keynote speaker, author, and team designer like you've never experienced before! He helps leaders to engage their teams through purposeful and entertaining team building by using measurable design and focused tools.

Tyler has been an internationally respected team builder, author, and corporate speaker since 1996. He delivers a powerful punch that inspires teams, innovates management techniques, and invigorates team culture. When it comes to empowering audiences and teams to succeed—and to be their best every day—Tyler leads the way with insight and laughter.

He is the author of over 25 books and tools, and the creative mind behind 100s of powerful, downloadable, and fun team-building products available at www.teambuildingactivities.com. His live team-building events and motivational keynotes receive rave reviews from managers and business leaders alike with organizations such as TD Bank, G+D, YPO, WPO, PMI, Irving Oil, Michelin, Parmalat, Red Cross, ExxonMobil, and more.

Tyler's work-life balance practice of Livin' Life Large™ and team tool of Multiple Intelligence Quotient methodology has informed his lifestyle, leadership, and team-building work since 1996 as well, guiding the various small businesses he operates.

Finally, a description of Tyler would not be complete without a word about his greatest sources of affluence: family and community. Tyler is a loving and proud father of Tait and Breton, his beautiful girls. He served as an elected official for Lunenburg, Nova Scotia. Tyler looks forward to continuing to build a loving family and to making a difference in his quiet seaside community and beyond.

Discover more at www.tylerhayden.com and www.teambuildingactivities.com.

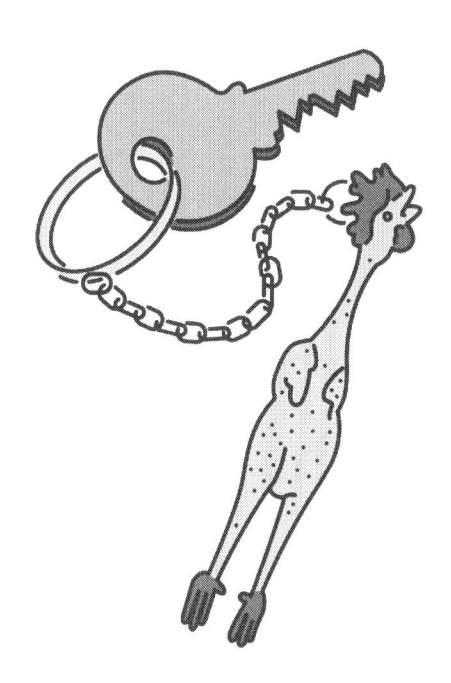

Manufactured by Amazon.ca
Bolton, ON